Simple Steps

to

Growing Your Donors

Simple Steps

to

Growing Your Donors

by Kirsten M. Bullock, CFRE

The Nonprofit Academy

This book is dedicated to those who are
giving their lives away in pursuit of
a better world.

A special thank you to my husband Rob
for encouraging me, loving me and
inspiring me to be my best.

Table of Contents

Introduction

When I started as a Development Director twelve years ago, I wished that there was a book like this one. One that would provide an overview of a development program and help me step-by-step through the process. After I completed developing an online training program, I realized that I had all the content to develop that book for others who are new to the field. I hope this book will help you grow a sustainable fundraising program that will allow you to serve those in need of your assistance. I also hope that it will help make advanced fundraising strategies available to organizations that may not otherwise be able to access those strategies.

Before we dive in to the technical aspects of fundraising, there is one thing I need to say - if there's just one thing you remember from this book, I hope that it's this: that fundraising is really an honor – it's a privilege. And it's not about the money.

As development professionals, we get to help make people's dreams come true. People come – with funds that they want to give to a good cause – and with causes that they're passionate about and goals that they want to accomplish. They are able to do accomplish their goals and dreams through the programs nonprofit organizations offer. It's truly an honor and a privilege to work with donors to help them accomplish their life goals (and help our community at the same time). It's really about the mission – and not about the money.

About Kirsten

When I was growing up, I didn't dream about becoming a fundraising professional. I'm pretty sure I didn't even know that it was a possibility.

I was introduced to nonprofits from a very young age and spent ten summers, from age 2 to age 12, at a camp for kids with physical disabilities (my father was the camp director and my mom the camp nurse). That experience, combined with having a brother with Duchenne Muscular Dystrophy, had a profound impact on my life. It taught me to not make assumptions about people based on what I could see. And, it taught me that there are lots of ways we can help make the world a better place.

It was at an Arts school in North Carolina, while majoring in Stage Management, when I was first introduced to philanthropy. My work study assignment was in the Foundation. Four years later, when I was working towards my Bachelors degree in social work, I completed my internship at the foundation at a local hospital. There were so many people committed to doing what they could to help insure that people in our community had access to the most advanced health care possible. I was hooked.

After taking a break to complete my Masters in Business, I returned to nonprofits as the development director for a community health center. It was there that I experienced the thrill of growing a development program from the ground up. In a three-year time period, we went from $200,000 to $1,378,249 in grants and charitable gifts raised.

Since that time, I've had the honor and privilege to work with over two dozen organizations in various capacities. These have ranged from small local startups to multi-million dollar organizations.

Now, in my role as a fundraising coach, I strive to make the strategies used in established fundraising programs (ie hospitals and universities) available to those organizations with smaller budgets (but just as big aspirations!). My hope is that this book will provide you with the tools you need to meet the needs of the communities you serve.

An Introduction to Philanthropy

Fundraising means so many different things to different people. Growing up, most of us were exposed to 'fundraising' drives where we sold cookies or chocolate or wrapping paper. As we grow up, we start getting invited to fundraising events. We purchase a ticket and get to attend an event of some sort (the galas and golf tournaments). Then there are the 'thons – the walkathons, bikeathons. No wonder, for many people, 'fundraising' has become a very transactional experience. It's no longer about the mission of the organization, but about how we can sell things to earn the money to run the organization. For other people, fundraising is about begging, arm twisting and manipulating people in to giving a gift.

When I say fundraising, I'm thinking more about Philanthropy. According to the Merriam-Webster dictionary, this means: "goodwill to fellow members of the human race; *especially*: active effort to promote human welfare."

Under this definition, philanthropy is an investment in our community and our society by people who want to have an impact and give back in some way. So fundraising (or promoting philanthropy) becomes more about finding people who are passionate about our cause and who want to promote human welfare through the organization we are working with.

Obstacles

Even recognizing this, there are many obstacles that can get in the way of an organization being able to effectively address community issues because of a lack of funding. Some of the issues that come to mind immediately include a lack of community awareness about the organization, not being connected to the right people who have the ability to give a large gift and not having the systems in place to keep contributors informed about how their gifts are being put to good use.

Awareness of the need. As a 'newbie' to the nonprofit field some 15 years ago, I was a little frustrated by the lack of interest community leaders and those with wealth seemed to have in the issues that I saw as being important. Through a local leadership program, I came to understand that it wasn't that people didn't care, they just didn't know. So we need to do a better job of presenting the needs in the community. We also need to let the community know that the organization is there addressing the challenges the community is facing. We don't want to be our community's 'best-kept secret.'

Connections. In fundraising, we often talk about the importance of linkage, ability and interest. Linkage means that the organization is connected to the potential contributor in some way. Ability refers to the ability to make a significant gift to the organization. Finally, interest refers to the person having some interest in the cause. It's all about finding the right people, not just everybody.

Communication. Hopefully, it won't come as a surprise to you that people who contribute to our organizations want to know how things are going. They want to know that they've been able to impact people's lives as a result of your work. One study has found that not enough appropriate communication is the leading cause of contributors choosing to not give again. Through email and social media, this has become significantly easier.

Overview of This Book

This book will cover the basics of starting, or growing, a fundraising program for your organization.

The first chapter will provide an overview of the state of giving in the United States as well as an overview of a fundraising program. The next chapter contains information to help you review your vision and the mission. The vision is really the core of your fundraising program (if we don't know where we're going, it's hard to convince other people to come alongside us and join us in the cause). Therefore having your vision clear will make raising major gifts much easier.

The case statement is the document that you'll be taking out with you when you meet with major gift prospects to talk with them about the organization and the role you are hoping they will play in it. A better name for it could be 'Your Story.' The case statement encapsulates the vision and mission, along with information about the programs, organization and leadership of the organization. It also includes information about how the money will be spent and how the community will be positively impacted.

During the audience section, we'll talk about narrowing your focus down to specific groups of people – as well as specific individuals. Be prepared to think about specific people and how you might approach them.

Awareness will cover many different strategies you might use to raise awareness of your organization. It will also help you focus in on those specific people you are trying to reach.

The next chapter will include information about inviting people to join in your efforts, primarily by asking for a gift. This will focus in on sitting down in-person with someone to ask for a gift. We'll also talk about cultivation strategies. Rarely will you ask for a large gift on a first visit. You'll need to spend some time getting to know your potential donor and make sure that your organization is a good fit for them and their philanthropic goals.

In the seventh chapter we'll be talking about the fundraising plan –pulling it all together. That includes everything from the first six weeks and creating a plan with everything broken down in to a specific time frame with assignments related to who has responsibilities for each step.

And then, finally, the last chapter: working with volunteers and staff. This will include recruiting people to work with you on the fundraising plan as well as engaging your organization's board of directors to work with you (on both developing and implementing the plan.

There is one recurring theme that I hope you will notice as we go through these materials: everything needs to be <u>donor</u>-centered rather than organization-centered. Fundraising is primarily about helping our donors accomplish <u>their</u> life goals.

ONE: State of Giving in the US

The first step in any large endeavor is to understand the environment you are operating in. As you'll see from the information in this chapter, people are very generous.

Giving USA reports are prepared annually with data from tax returns of charitable organizations. It is now collaboration between the Giving USA Foundation and The Center on Philanthropy at Indiana University.

These numbers have been fairly consistent since 1985, when the report was first published.

In 2010, we see that the majority of gifts in the United States come from individuals (a total of 83% when you add bequests to individuals giving. Foundations made up 14% of total gifts and corporations were responsible for about 5%.

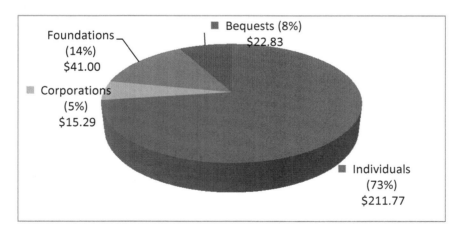

Source: *Giving USA 2011: The Annual Report on Philanthropy for the Year 2010*

Trends in Giving

From 1970 to 2006, there were a few times we saw giving, in inflation-adjusted dollars, decrease. However 2008 was just the second time since Giving USA began tracking these numbers that giving in real dollars decreased (the first was in 1987). In 2009, giving decreased again. But 2010 saw a slight uptick n giving. While we are seeing signs that giving is on an upward trend again, we are not yet (in July 2011) back to pre-recession levels yet. Here is a graph, in five-year increments that provides some more information on this.

Trends in Total Giving: 1970 – 2010
(in billions of dollars)

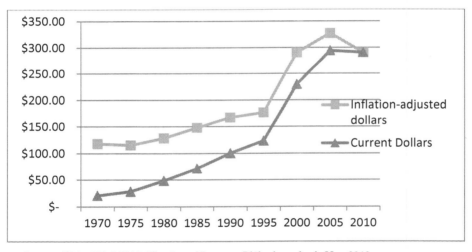

Source: *Giving USA 2011: The Annual Report on Philanthropy for the Year 2010*

Another way to look at giving over time is to compare it to Gross Domestic Product. Over time, this seems to correlate most closely to giving. From 1970 to 2010, giving has ranged from 1.7% to 2.4% of GDP.

Giving as a percentage of Gross Domestic Product (GDP), 1970 – 2010

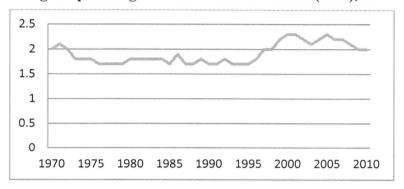

Source: *Giving USA 2011: The Annual Report on Philanthropy for the Year 2010*

Over the last 40 years, we've become much more sophisticated with our fundraising strategies, but not seeing any increase in giving related to GDP.

Fundraising Effectiveness Project

Overall giving history can only tell us so much. A project that was initiated just a few years ago, the Fundraising Effectiveness Project, provides some information I find much more useful for the fundraising practitioner. The goal of the Fundraising Effectiveness Project is to help organizations increase the effectiveness of their fundraising program thereby increasing giving overall.

One of the unique things about this ongoing study is its partnership with donor management software providers. With permission, the software companies provide aggregate information to the study. Because the software providers make it easy for their clients to submit data for the annual survey, data can be collected and compiled fairly easily. The data on the next two slides represents 1,982 responses.

What they found when looking at the results of the study, was that while new dollars were being generated, existing donors renewed at such a low rate that the result was a net loss in revenue generated.

The 45% increase in the dollar value of gifts was offset by a decrease of 61.1% in giving by existing donors yielding a net loss of 8.1% in revenue from charitable gifts.

2008 – 2009 – Overall Growth in Giving

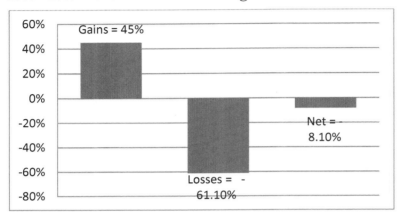

Source: 2010 Fundraising Effectiveness Survey Report

The study also found that there was also a net loss in the number of donors contributing to organizations represented in this study.

Overall, the organizations saw an increase of 52% in new and recaptured donors. But new and repeat donors were discontinuing their giving at a higher rate. The average net loss in donors was .8%.

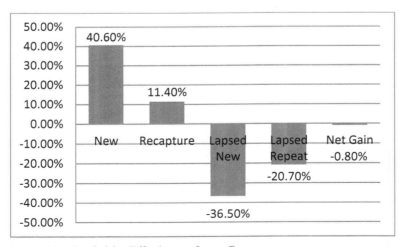

Source: 2010 Fundraising Effectiveness Survey Report

As you can see, we're doing a great job of finding new donors, we need to do a much better job of keeping the donors who have already told us that they're passionate about the work our organization is doing. This is primarily accomplished through communications strategies which we'll be covering in detail in Module 4.

First-Steps in Developing a Fundraising Program

If you've been to any fundraising training, I'm sure you've seen this illustration before.

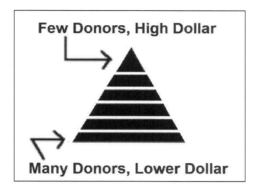

It's probably safe to say that most organizations haven't been able to make their donor pyramid this clean. Some are more slanted towards smaller donors – resulting in higher fundraising costs. Others have a larger number of donors making major gifts – resulting in potential instability of the organization if two or three of those donors decide to leave. Several organizations I've seen lately have been lean in the middle, leaving them at risk of not building relationships that will result in high dollar gifts down the road.

It is, however, a good ideal to strive for: a large number of smaller donors (some of who become prospects for mid-level gifts), a moderate number of givers at intermediate amounts (some of whom become prospects for major gifts), and a few donors who give large amounts. This helps to assure that as donors migrate away, there will be others ready to step in at higher levels.

Essential Components

In the organizations I've worked with, ones that have successful fundraising programs have these five things in common. While we won't be covering each of them in-depth in this book, I thought it a good idea to at least mention them up front.

Board Led – The board sets the 'tone at the top.' if the board is on-board, so to speak, others will be much more likely to follow. This applies to both a time and a financial commitment.

Mission / Vision Driven – In Alice in Wonderland, the caterpillar says that if you don't know where you're going, any road will get you there. The vision describes how the community will be impacted as a result of the work you do. The mission will keep everyone in the organization focused on the same goal by clarifying how that vision will be accomplished.

Donor-Centered – The days of people giving money to an institution because they trust that the money will be well-spent are slowly coming to a close. It makes sense to move towards helping donors define their passion and personal goals, and then help them accomplish those goals through our organization. At a shelter for homeless youth many years ago, I met a woman who cared deeply about homeless youth. At one time, she had invited more than one homeless youth to stay in her home. It didn't take long for her to realize that she was ill-equipped to handle the challenges those kids faced. So it made sense for her to partner with the organization I was working for.

Donors want to know that the organization is having an impact on the community. And, more frequently, they want to become involved in the work or the organization, rather than just writing a check. So those organizations that engage people in meaningful ways will come out ahead.

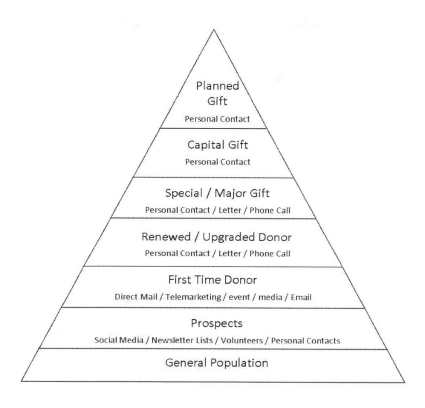

This is a more detailed view of the donor pyramid – with a few additional levels added in. One of the primary things to remember about this chart is that it represents an 'ideal' in the industry – it won't necessarily be illustrative of how yours will eventually look. The second is that a few people at each level will most likely end up wanting to move to the next level.

I've added a level at the bottom of the chart. The general population represents those people we hope may want to become involved with our cause. They don't become prospects until we've seen some evidence that they want to become more involved. And, there are several ways that can happen. They might volunteer to help at an event, sign up for your email newsletter list, sign a petition, sign up as 'liking' your Facebook page, or any other myriad of ways.

Some will most likely become donors (if they're asked appropriately). Then some of those will renew their gifts, some of those will upgrade their gift, and eventually a handful will give a major gift or a capital gift.

It's interesting to note that about 40% of people who give planned gifts to an organization have been contributing to the organization for 7 or more years.

A sustainable fundraising program will need to include both annual and major gifts. Here are some of the differences:

Annual Gifts	Major Gifts
• Higher cost per $ raised	• Lower cost per $ raised
• Lower dollar amounts	• Higher dollar amounts
• From current income	• From investments
• Impersonal ask	• Personal ask
• Used for operating costs	• Used for special projects
• Begins habit of giving	• One-time gifts
• Prospect list for larger gifts	

Annual gifts have a higher cost per dollar raised while major gifts have a lower cost (but remember that major gift prospects typically come from your pool of annual givers. So while there are some ways to jump start a major gifts program, it will not be sustainable unless you start building a pool of prospects for future major gifts).

Annual gifts are lower dollar amounts and are typically made from current income, while major gifts might come from the assets of a donor (sometimes investments or from the sale of a property).

Annual gifts are made in response to an impersonal ask – such as a direct mail piece, phone call or email. Major gifts rely on asking for the gift in person and are typically for a specific project.

For a major gifts program to succeed, we need to get a lot of things 'right.'

It's the right person asking the right prospect for the right amount in the right way at the right time for the right cause with the right follow-up. This depends on an approach that is donor-focused to help us determine what those right things might be.

Encouraging Predictions Regarding Giving

Annually, the Cygnus Donor Survey is completed. The 2011 survey found some encouraging news. Here are some of the findings:

Younger donors planned to give more. Donors (age 35 and younger) were more likely to say that they planned to contribute a higher dollar amount and to more organizations this year.

Majority of donors were giving at the same levels or higher. 80% of respondents reported that they had given the same amount or more in 2010 as compared to 2009.

Donor loyalty was related to reputation, trustworthiness and showing measurable results. Reputation and trustworthiness of the organization were most closely tied to donor loyalty (53% of respondents also indicated that measurable results were important).

Here are some other findings:

- o Interest in direct mail was waning. Only 1% of respondents indicated that they planned on giving more through direct mail (due to over solicitation and excessive cost).
- o Interest in online communications / social media continued to rise.
- o More people reported that they were giving online
- o 69% indicated that they preferred electronic communications
- o 17% of social media account holders reported having made a first-time gift to an organization after following them
- o Social media users who follow charities gave 28% less than their non-charity following social media user counterparts

Available at: http://www.cygresearch.com/cds2011/

A Simplified Four-Step Model for Asking For Gifts

That leads us to a simplified, and respectful, model for asking for a gift. We introduce people to our cause. I advocate what I refer to as 'as you go' fundraising. As board members (and staff) go through their day and interact with people, they make a point of mentioning something about the cause of the organization. Some people will show absolutely no interest. And that's fine. However, others will ask more questions and will self-identify as wanting more information.

For those who are interested, we involve them in some way with the organization. It could be through volunteering or in-kind gifts. Ministries may want to establish a prayer team (if they haven't already).

Then, at some point (based in the fundraising plan in place), invite them to contribute financially. This is 'the ask.' People don't know that there's a need unless we ask. And they won't give unless they know there's a need.

Finally, repeat. Continue to provide information and feedback. And, occasionally, ask again. Remember that marketing theory states that people need to hear something seven times before they remember it. So this could be a good rule of thumb – say thank you seven times before asking for another gift.

Key Points

- Fundraising is not begging. Rather, it's inviting people to be part of something that they are already passionate about.
- People are generous. In the US in 2009, $303.75 billion was given in charitable contributions.
- We need to learn how to do a better job of keeping our current donors – primarily by keeping them informed about and engaged in the work of the organization.
- A strong annual giving program is typically a precursor to a major gift program.
- It really doesn't need to be complicated. We introduce, involve, invite and repeat.

TWO: Vision, Mission, Plan

I'm sure you've heard the stories too – people and groups who accomplish amazing things that others said couldn't be done. These stories happen in urban areas, rural areas, by large groups, small groups, and sometimes individuals. One thing then have in common is that they knew where they were trying to get to.

The vision of the organization is probably the most important aspect of planning an organization can do (as well as the most misunderstood). While many people have different definitions of what a vision, mission and strategic plan, here are the concepts that I'm guided by:

The vision of the organization involves defining what the community would look like in 10, 25 or 50 years, as a result of our work. This is NOT about your organization and what it will look like. Rather, it is about the community you serve and how it will be impacted. In many ways the vision could be considered the why of your work.

The mission, on the other hand, is the what. For example - bringing safe drinking water to the community, giving kids an alternative to hanging out on the street or helping build a stronger community.

The plan defines how it will happen. It covers information about the specific programs and costs – for example staff, infrastructure and buildings.

There are two ways to go about this process. One way is to start with the activities and then define the mission and vision based on that. However – I prefer to start with the end in mind (as Steve Covey likes to say). So we'll start with the vision first.

What's Your Vision?

When someone plants a Coco-de-mer palm tree, they have a vision that is literally decades in to the future. The Coco-de-mer palm tree takes 25 years to reach maturity and start bearing fruit – which take an additional 7 years to mature.

So what's your 32-year vision for your organization? What if it were to go out of business? No. Really. What if you did your job so well that the challenge you're addressing is no longer an issue? If that were your goal, would it change how you work today? Or is it too audacious to even consider?

A vision, to be really compelling, to engage everyone around you, should be something audacious. As you think about it, does your heart start to race? Are you thinking, "maybe it's really a possibility?"

But then perhaps there's a naysayer in your organization who tells you all the reasons it can't happen. Or there's nagging doubt in the back of your mind. But it can happen. And nonprofits can lead the way in making it happen.

- The March of Dimes was instrumental in developing the vaccine to end epidemic polio in the United States (and has since expanded their mission to be stronger, healthier babies).
- The work of MADD helped us, as a society, see drunk driving as unacceptable.
- Charity: Water, through use of social media and traditional communications outlets, has been able to provide drinking water in developing nations (reached over one million people in 2009).

Each of these organizations started small. Each had (and have) a clear vision of what they want to accomplish.

So, what's your vision?

Some Examples

Here are a few examples of what I'm talking about. The first is an international program and the other two examples are from local programs.

CHARITY: WATER

The first example we're going to look at is for an organization called Charity: Water. It's a relative newcomer in the nonprofit world, but has definitely made an impact.

Feel free to take a moment to visit their webpage at www.charitywater.org and watch their promotional video. It seems that every time I watch it I recognize another thing that they have done right. The video is not about the organization – it's about people having access to clean water.

Vision: Now we'll look at the vision of Charity: Water (accessed in March 2011):

> "charity: water served its first one million people at the end of 2009. That's a major accomplishment, but we have much more work to do. By 2050, the world's population is estimated to grow by three billion and 90% of this growth will be in the developing world. Unless sustainable water solutions are scaled fast, regions already stressed for safe water sources will be over capacity. We're expanding our reach to meet these demands and will not stop until every person has safe water to drink."

Mission: Their mission is clearly stated on their home page: Charity:water brings clean and safe drinking water to people in developing nations. Because Charity:water obtains large designated gifts to cover their overhead costs, they are able to say that 100% of their public donations go directly to fund water projects.

Plan: In order to have a well thought-out plan, it's important to recognize the needs that the community has. In the case of Charity: Water, they center around three main issues: Health &Sanitation, women & children, economies / communities. Specifics are outlined on their 'Why Water?' page.

The Needs Statement is probably the second most important part of a funding proposal to an individual (through a case statement) or a foundation (through a grant proposal). It illustrates a thorough understanding of the constituency and helps to educate people on the real needs of the community. We can't assume that everyone knows about the issues faced by the people we serve.

While we are not covering the Needs Statement in depth in this chapter, I introduce it so that you can start to think about what three primary needs you are meeting in the community. Go ahead and start gathering some statistics and data related to those needs.

Charity: Water's plan is to, in partnership with local communities, build hand-dug wells, drilled wells, rehabilitation of existing wells, spring protections, rainwater catchments, and BioSand filters. On their projects page, Charity:Water also outlines their progress so far (as of March 2011, 3,811 water projects serving 1,742,331 people).

CENTER FOR MULTICULTURAL WELLNESS AND PREVENTION (www.cmwp.org)

This next example is a fairly small organization having a large impact. The majority of their funding comes from government contracts, but they've also been building up some support from the private community.

I met the executive director of CMWP (or the Center for Multicultural Wellness and Prevention) about 12 years ago when I served as the development director for a group of community health centers in central Florida.

Vision: Their vision statement is clearly stated on their 'About Us' page: "a Central Florida without health disparities and 100% access to services."

Mission: Their mission is clearly stated on their 'About Us' page: "To enhance the quality of life for diverse and ethnic populations through the provision of health promotion services."

Plan: The programs that CMWP offers currently center around education and awareness for the following issues:

- Project CONNECT - Asthma Education
- Heart & Soul - Cardiovascular Disease Prevention / Diabetes and Obesity
- Cancer Awareness - colorectal and breast cancer
- Project
- Ryan White Title I - health management
- NYELA - SISTA CDC Intervention - HIV/AIDS awareness program for women
- HOPWA - Housing Opportunity for People with AIDS
- AWARE - breast cancer education and awareness

AIDS INTERFAITH MINISTRIES OF KENTUCKIANA

The final example we'll look at today is another local organization. My accountant introduced me to them a couple of years ago.

AIM was established about 20 years ago and helps people living with HIV/AIDS.

Vision: The vision of AIM centers around building a supportive community:

- Eliminating the stigma of living with HIV/AIDS
- Increasing compassion and volunteer support
- Preventing the spread of HIV AIDS

Mission: AIM is committed to helping people living with HIV/AIDS by providing nutritional, emotional and spiritual support. We offer community, dignity and hope.

Plan: Their plan for accomplishing this vision and mission is to provide the following programs at no charge:

- Counseling
- Lifeskills educational workshops
- Support groups
- Grief, bereavement and pastoral care
- Monthly Fellowship dinners (in partnership with another ministry)
- Annual spiritual retreats
- Food pantry
- Personal care items
- Household cleaning supplie
- Bed, bath and kitchen starter kits
- Non-HIV medication assistance

Developing a Shared Vision

Before you begin writing your vision, I'd like to take some time to review some general thoughts related to vision. These are primarily inspired by The Leadership Challenge by Kouzes and Posner.

The Leadership Challenge

Kouzes and Posner advocate a five-step process for leaders to inspire change in an organization. These are premises that many follow, whether or not they are familiar with The Leadership challenge.

The first is to Model the Way. Leaders establish the 'tone at the top' so to speak.

The second is inspiring a shared vision. It means expanding the creation of a vision to a much larger group of people than typically dream up the vision. Because being part of the creation of the vision helps to establish ownership, the result is more lasting and inspires a higher commitment to the cause.

The third is to challenge the process. Just because something isn't broken doesn't necessarily mean that there might be a better way to do it.

Next is enabling others to act. No control freaks allowed! According to Expert Magazine, The Ritz empowers their employees to spend up to $2,000 to 'bring instant resolution to a guest's problem. Guest satisfaction is the top priority – and you won't hear an employee say – 'that's not my job.'

Finally, encouraging the heart. We need to take time to celebrate accomplishments and celebrate each other.

There are two steps The Leadership Challenge advocates to inspire a shared vision.

The first is to "envision the future by imagining exciting and ennobling possibilities." I encourage you to spend some time writing down your thoughts about your organization's vision. Your vision might cause your heart to race and your hands to sweat – because it's that exciting, that impossible, and that needed.

The second is to "enlist others in a common vision by appealing to shared aspirations." The vision inspires us to want to do something – and is based in shared values.

The vision statement calls us to a higher purpose. Shared aspirations unite us. It's only when we share the same vision and aspirations will we can effectively pull together to achieve common goals.

So why bother with a vision? We know what needs to be done – and people need help. Why do we need to spend time talking about it? We should just go out and help, right? Well – not so fast.

Spiritual

An ancient proverb says: 'Without a vision, the people perish.' If a group is not united by a common vision (or a common goal) the likelihood of conflict and distrust within the group increases. Perhaps you've seen it – organizations that have lost sight of their common vision and begun creating silos and fiefdoms.

George Cladis, who wrote The Team Based Church says:

"The vision gives a context for the labor or service that goes beyond the mere doing of it. The vision inspires workers, envisioning a future that they want to see come about. It becomes for them a sacred mission, a cause that motivates them beyond money or prestige." p 23

Having grown up in Disney's shadow, I've always been intrigued by stories about Disney. One that I heard related to the building of the Magic Kingdom.

Walt Disney

As you may (or may not) know – the Magic Kingdom is built on a swamp. So you can imagine the discomfort of the workers – in the heat of the day, mosquitoes and other generally unpleasant 'swampiness' happening. The story goes that Disney wanted the workers to be inspired to continue building the park, so he wanted to make sure that the first thing that was built would be a symbol of all the dreams that would come true – of all the families that would have a magical time. So what do you think he built first?

If you chose Cinderella's Castle, you're right. Orlando folklore says that Disney built Cinderella's castle first.

Here are some things to keep in mind as you begin to develop your vision.

- It represents an ideal that we want to strive for
- It's unique to you and your organization
- It helps to have an image in mind – something that you can use to help share your vision with other people.
- It's something in the future
- It's something that we are working towards together

Here are just a few of the benefits of having a shared vision:

- Working together for a common goal produces a sense of satisfaction.
- It ensures that we are all committed to the same goal.

- We are unified in what we are doing.
- And it clarifies organizational values.

John F Kennedy

Below is an excerpt from a famous speech that many have referenced as an example of a clear and compelling vision. Perhaps you've heard this speech before. Perhaps you were even there in Houston Texas that day.

Kennedy's speech at Rice University, Houston, Texas. September 12, 1962.

> But if I were to say, my fellow citizens, that we shall send to the moon, 240,000 miles away from the control station in Houston, a giant rocket more than 300 feet tall, the length of this football field, made of new metal alloys, some of which have not yet been invented, capable of standing heat and stresses several times more than have ever been experienced, fitted together with a precision better than the finest watch, carrying all the equipment needed for propulsion, guidance, control, communications, food and survival, on an untried mission, to an unknown celestial body, and then return it safely to earth, reentering the atmosphere at speeds of over 25,000 miles per hour, causing heat about half that of the temperature of the sun—almost as hot as it is here today—and do all this, and do it right, and do it first before this decade is out, then we must be bold.

> I'm the one who is doing all the work, so we just want you to stay cool for a minute. [Laughter]

> However, I think we're going to do it, and I think that we must pay what needs to be paid. I don't think we ought to waste any money, but I think we ought to do the job. And this will be done in the decade of the sixties. It may be done while some of you are still here at school at this college and university. It will be done during the terms of office of some of the people who sit here on this platform. But it will be done. And it will be done before the end of this decade.

I am delighted that this university is playing a part in putting a man on the moon as part of a great national effort of the United States of America.

Many years ago the great British explorer George Mallory, who was to die on Mount Everest, was asked why did he want to climb it. He said, "Because it is there."

Well, space is there, and we're going to climb it, and the moon and the planets are there, and new hopes for knowledge and peace are there. And, therefore, as we set sail we ask God's blessing on the most hazardous and dangerous and greatest adventure on which man has ever embarked.

Thank you.

SOURCE: http://millercenter.org/scripps/archive/speeches/detail/3371

Key Points

- Your vision is not about what your organization does, it's about how your community will be different as a result of what you do.
- Developing a vision is best done by the leaders of your organization.
- People want to be connected with a cause that is bigger than themselves.

THREE: Your Case Statement

The case statement could more aptly be named 'Your Story.' It is meant to inspire people to give to your organization. It provides a vision of what is possible – with a donors help, support and partnership. After a potential donor reviews your case statement, they should have a pretty good idea of what you're doing, why it's important, why yours is the best organization to tackle the issue, and what they can do to help.

Why Is The Case Statement Important?

Harold J Seymour, noted fund-raising pioneer, said: "The case statement is the definitive piece of the whole campaign. It tells all that needs to be told, answers all the important questions, reviews the arguments for support, explains the proposed plan for raising the money, and shows how gifts may be made, and who the people are who vouch for the project, **and** who will give it leadership and direction." That's a lot for one document to do.

The Case Statement is a single document that outlines who the agency is, why it's important, what it does, how much it will cost and how people can help. In some ways it attempts to crystallize the essence of your organization. It also invites people to engage in the mission of the organization.

While the document is certainly an important component of your major gifts program, more important is the process of developing the ideas, concepts and goals of the organization. It's a great opportunity for the key stakeholders in your organization to revisit your shared vision of what the agency is and what it will become.

Here are a few uses of a case statement:

Builds consensus. First, when key stakeholders are engaged in the process, the development of the case helps to build consensus within the organization.

Source materials for other pieces. It can also be used as a source for all campaign materials – and perhaps for your annual campaign as well.

Feasibility Study. Before embarking on a major campaign, many organizations chose to complete a feasibility study to make sure that the project – and amount – is palatable to persons with the propensity to make large gifts. A case statement is used to convey information about the potential campaign to potential supporters.

Conveys organizational credibility. The case statement allows the organization to include information about why they are best suited to address the cause.

Inspirational. And finally (and why this is included in this training), it is essential in providing inspiration to donors who may want to give a major gift to your organization.

Why Don't They Care?

I remember thinking, 'why don't they care?' as I was working towards my social work degree. My classmates would come back from their internships and share about people living in poverty, in houses with gaping holes in the roof, ceiling and floor. Learning tips from those who had been in the field a long time. Things like: make sure you go early in the day before the trouble makers wake up. Avoid sitting on anything with cushions (to avoid lice and bugs). If you must sit on a cushion, sit as far forward as possible.

And all around me there were people who seemed to just not care. Have you ever gotten frustrated because others just don't seem to care about the work you are doing?

Let me help you with a little tip: it's not that they don't care. It's more typical that they just don't know. It's your job to educate them. Not in a way that's abrasive or condescending. Not by accusing or yelling or thinking less of them. But, by simply sharing your story in a way that helps them catch up.

As part of your 'case statement' include information about the community needs that are being addressed as a result of your work. This will include background information about how the issue started becoming a concern, what impact it is having in your community and statistics to back up what you've said. This helps build you and your organization as the experts and it provides back-up information to help educate people who do not have personal experience with the issue you address. In addition, it provides information for your advocates to share and helps simplify your messaging.

Who Develops the Case?

It might be tempting to just recruit someone (ie your development director or a volunteer) and just tell them to write the case. However, please keep in mind that this document summarizes everything about the organization, it's essential to have leadership involved in the development of these materials.

- Development Director (if there is one)
- Executive Director
- Other Key Staff
- Board Chair
- Board

Components of the Case Statement

Here are some general guidelines to keep in mind as you are compiling your materials.

- Stories are a great way to engage people, so include one or two
- Graphs and charts are ways to convey information in a simplified format – much better than including long dry paragraphs about data.
- A good picture is worth 1,000 words.
- White space makes it easier to read.
- The shorter the better – but it needs to be long enough to convey all of the important information.
- Keep it simple – avoid jargon and acronyms as much as possible.
- Each section of the case should communicate a sense of urgency - donors need to know that their help is needed now.
- And finally, plan on adapting this document for use with different constituents.

The quickest way to explain what a case statement does is say that it outlines how funding would be used. However, it is also a great opportunity to present all the essential things a potential donor might consider before making a gift to your organization to support your project. Keeping this in mind, the document includes these four sections:

- Need
- Program
- Qualifications
- Budget

Need

A common misperception of the needs statement is that it is about the needs of the organization. But it's really about the needs of the community. Focus on that and include data and citations to back up your claims. Stories about the challenges your constituency faces are helpful to illustrate this.

The Needs Statement is probably the most overlooked component of the case statement. The reason that it's so important is that if donor's don't know there's a problem, it will be very difficult to (1) develop any urgency around the campaign and (2) make the cause compelling. Don't assume that because you are passionate about the cause that everyone else knows that it's a cause to begin with.

And remember, the needs that are presented should relate to your programs - these are the issues that your program addresses and solves. So while you won't directly talk about your program here, it opens the door to do so in the next section.

Program

Recognizing that people really give to solutions – rather than needs, the Program section provides a picture of how things could be different. This is accomplished by sharing information about how your program works and how it will impact lives.

This section should include an overview of how your program operates and who it will serve. The goals and objectives that you talk about should reflect how lives will be changed and relate to the needs presented in the prior section.

Qualifications

The Agency Section provides information about your organization and illustrates all of the reasons you are uniquely suited to run programs to address the need highlighted in the first section. This includes your vision, philosophy, organization's history and information about your leaders (both board and key staff members).

As you develop information in each of these areas, keep in mind that they should help to answer the question, 'why you.' In addition, if you're always saying that you're the best-kept secret in town, include those best-kept secrets here.

Budget

Next is **the cost**. This section includes all of the financial information related to the program and the campaign. This includes the program and organizational budgets, your total fundraising goal, and a little about your fundraising plan.

EXERCISE:

Start to develop you case statement by taking these header sections (The Need, Agency, Cost, etc) and creating a document. Then start filling each section in. The total length of this document, in most cases shouldn't be longer than four pages.

Key Points

- The case statement shares the story of your organization.
- It's not that people don't care, it's more likely that they just don't know.
- Focus on the needs of your community – rather than the needs of your organization.

FOUR: Audiences

A few years ago, I made a really big mistake. I was working with a group that was putting together a presentation for an international audience. With a diverse audience like that, it can be really difficult to build the right message. Not thinking things through completely, when one of the principals with the group suggested that we use comedy, I said 'great idea!' Needless to say, it bombed. Humor does not translate well with a group from diverse cultures (who have different definitions of what is funny — and what isn't) and who don't share the same primary language.

I can't emphasize enough how important it is to know who you're talking to so that you can avoid a situation like that one.

Potential Audiences

In this first section, we'll cover general characteristics of individuals, companies, family businesses, foundations, etc. As you develop your awareness and fundraising strategies, it will be important to break this down further (for example, individuals who have incomes over $150,000 who are involved in the community, are connected to your organization in some way and who live within 10 miles of your location). Regardless of the type of audience you are looking at, there are three important things to keep in mind:

- **Linkage.** Most gifts to organizations do not come from strangers. They come from people who are connected to, or linked to, your organization in some way. Board members and volunteers are typically the closest linked. The clients themselves, family members, vendors, companies that might benefit indirectly from what you do and the community around your physical location are some categories that might apply to your organization.
- **Ability.** Next, especially with major gifts, you want to identify whether or not those individuals (or groups) have the ability to

make a large gift to your organization. This can be accomplished with a focus group – maybe some members of your board with some additional community leaders – or through paid research. There are 'prospect researchers' who can compile a portfolio of information about each of your potential donors. In addition, there are companies that will complete a 'wealth screening' to help you identify people in your current donor pool who have the ability to give larger gifts.

- **Interest.** Do they have any interest in your cause? Just because they are connected and have the ability doesn't mean that they're interested. As you develop your major gift program, you'll likely be meeting with people individually to help determine whether your organization is the right one to fulfill the donor's philanthropic goals. If it's not a good fit, they might know others who would be (don't forget to ask that question). With overall giving programs, social media has given us new ways to let potential givers express interest in our cause. Facebook pages, Twitter, LinkedIn pages, Causes, etc.

Individuals

There are very few organizations that won't benefit by having individuals as a component of their philanthropic efforts (83% of charitable gifts come from individuals). Individuals are also more likely to continue their support over time – if they are kept informed about how their gifts are being used. Another benefit is that givers also become advocates (and vice versa). The majority of volunteers also donate, so if you're not occasionally asking your volunteers for support it's something to consider.

For all that, there are still some disadvantages to seeking individual support. It can be costly to develop. Most acquisition strategies barely cover the cost of the initial appeal (the value in having a new donor is in engaging the giver for the long-term). It can be difficult (and expensive) to reach large numbers of potential donors. In addition, individual giving requires extensive commitment and assistance from your board and volunteers.

Large Family Foundations

For the right organization and the right program, large family foundations can be a good source of funding (however, most large family foundations will not support the same program for more than three years). And while they might have a lot of money to give away, they typically have very strict guidelines about the programs they are looking for. They also often have lengthy application forms and processes that need to be followed.

Many of the larger foundations have professional staff who can answer questions and help guide you through the process – don't be afraid to pick up the phone and call them. Relationships with board members might help, but it's important to recognize that some foundations frown on that approach (when that is the case it is typically made clear somewhere in their printed materials).

Community Foundations

Community foundations can be similar to large family foundations, in that they have staff, clear guidelines, etc. However the funds they hold are typically run like mini-foundations themselves, so you really need to be reaching out to the fund holders, rather than the community foundation itself. But, as a community foundation executive I know said, if you know one community foundation, you know one community foundation. They are each unique in the way they operate.

Small Family Foundations

If you've looked through any foundation directories, you've probably seen many listings that indicate the foundation does not accept unsolicited proposals. This is often the case for small family foundations. They may fund ongoing operating expenses (and sometimes for a long period of time), their guidelines are broad and there is much flexibility with the application format. However, it is essential to have a direct connection to a trustee or board member as they typically do not have professional staff. In addition, grant amounts are typically smaller than other foundations.

Large Corporations / Corporate Foundations

In the last few years, cause-related marketing has made the news, and more frequently, company-sponsored contests that award large dollar amounts to a few organizations (I can sometimes be a little cynical and this latter trend seems to me more like a way to get a lot of free advertising at the expense of non-profit organizations).

Large companies can be a source for large sums of money. In some cases, they will also fund operating costs (at a smaller level) on an ongoing basis. They will often have professional staff committed to support their granting efforts. Having volunteers from the company involved in your organization can be helpful. With corporate giving, grants are typically tied to a direct business strategy, so it's important to understand what the company is hoping to accomplish through their giving.

Here are a few things to keep in mind. Large sums of money from corporations will not be ongoing. It may be difficult to speak directly to the people who actually make the giving decisions. As with large foundations, corporate giving program generally have very specific guidelines about the programs they fund. This may include representation on your board and having a presence in the community you serve.

Small Businesses

Small businesses are ideal prospects for local sponsorships at lower dollar levels. As with small family foundations, personal relationships are essential. Funding can be ongoing and a neighborhood focus helps. A few things that local businesses love: their logos on t-shirts and a plaque they can put in their window to let their customers know about the causes they are involved with.

Federated Funds (United Ways, United Arts, Etc.)

Over the past few years, gift through federated campaigns have been declining. Very few federated giving programs are accepting new agencies. However, for those established agencies that qualify, federated campaigns can be a steady source of relatively large sums of money. They typically have a clear application process (though lengthy) with professional staff on-hand to answer questions and help guide you through the process. In addition to the application process, there is a requirement that participating agencies be active in the annual fundraising process for the fund.

Government

A few years ago there were commercials that talked about how easy it was to get grants from the government. That really couldn't be further from the truth. While it is possible to obtain large sums of money, the application process is both intense and competitive. In many cases, they will only reimburse based on units of service (that may or may not actually cover the cost of providing that service). With that said, it can be a source of ongoing funding and the application process is clear. It should go without saying, but following directions during the application process is essential. More often than not, applications that are not in compliance with the directions won't even get reviewed.

Churches, Temples and Community Groups

An organization I was involved with several years ago was adopted by one of the larger churches in our area as their Christmas project. Through their efforts, the organization received over $30,000 worth of items (including gift cards, socks, backpacks, etc.) and was exposed to over 4,000 people. While churches, temples and community groups may not directly represent large gifts, reaching out to these communities are great ways to engage the members who are part of them. They are typically looking for group projects that could include things like painting, yard work, volunteering at an event, or collecting in-kind items that your organization can use.

5 Questions to Help You Identify Potential Supporters

So, you want to have a major gift campaign. While there are some groups that are able to jump right in to major gifts, most nonprofits have to do some preparation first - primarily in the area of building a core group of supporters who have the ability to give major gifts.

Here are five questions you can ask that will help you identify some people and companies who have the ability to provide significant support for your organization.

1. Who in your community is interested in the issue you're addressing? Keep an eye on your local newspapers. Do you have a business journal published in your area? Definitely keep an eye on that as well. It would be natural for you to call them up to compare notes and explore ways you might be able to work together.

2. Who benefits if your goal is accomplished? Will there be more prepared workers entering the workforce? Will an area of town be cleaned up (and more appealing to investors)? Find out who will benefit. Then call them and talk.

3. Who are you connected to personally? Take a good look at your contact list(s). If you're not personally connected to someone with the potential to make a significant gift, chances are that you are connected with someone who is. Buy them coffee. Talk about what you're up to. Explore whether or not they'd be comfortable making an introduction - or if they might have some knowledge of whether the person has an interest in your cause.

4. Are there businesses that would like to look good in front of your constituents? Many local businesses will hang plaques in their places of business about their charitable involvement. It's an avenue to explore.

5. What community leaders could you connect with? You'd be surprised at the numbers of people who will freely give advice to those who ask (sometimes it will take multiple calls / emails for someone to call you back, but don't give up!)

Who Are You Connected To?

Now that we've covered some of the potential audiences of your organization, let's talk about those groups you are already connected to. Below is a sample of a 'Circle of Connections' chart. Feel free to use this format or come up with your own. But please don't just copy what this one says. Ideally you'll want to pull together a group of people who are involved with your organization to help you identify those individuals, groups and companies you're already connected to.

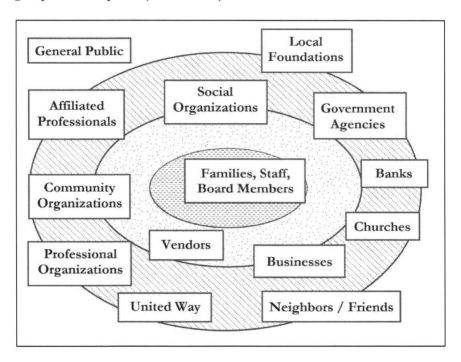

Narrowing your audience

These are some fairly broad categories. Now that you have a better idea of who you are connected to, I'd like to suggest some steps you can take to better define what your potential donors might look like.

One good way is to talk with your current donors to find out more about them. Chances are that other people, who are similar to them, may also want to contribute to your organization. Find out what they read, where they spend their time and what they like to do in their spare time. This can be accomplished through a survey or, better yet, pick up the phone a call them.

You can also look up information about other organizations that are similar to yours and see what type of people, groups and companies are giving to them. If you're not sure where to start, visit www.guidestar.org and do a search to find them. A lot of information can be gathered by looking at their websites and reading articles about them. In addition to looking at donor information, you can also compare financial information (from a fundraising perspective t could be helpful to look at total dollars raised by source and fundraising expenses versus fundraising income).

With the technology that is available to us today, it's easier to target communications based on user preferences. The more information you collect in your database the easier this will be.

Segmenting Your Audiences

Here are some thoughts about how you can segment your donors. This is important information to gather as you try to find out what they read and where they hang out.

Perhaps there's a magazine that is geared towards your potential donors that you can get as a media sponsor for an event – or a place that people gather that will share information on your behalf.

• Age	• Ethnic background
• Location	• Personality
• Gender	• Attitudes
• Income level	• Values
• Education level	• Interests / hobbies
• Marital/family status	• Lifestyles
• Occupation	• Behavior

Research to Determine Market Size / Viability

Before moving forward, it's important to confirm that there are enough potential donors in a group to structure a campaign around them. Here are a few sources you can look at to help determine that.

- www.InfoUSA.com – search for mailing lists, ID potential target size
- David Lamb's Prospect Research Page: http://home.comcast.net/~lambresearch/index.html
- www.Guidestar.org
- Libraries with Foundation Center Resources (Cooperating Collections) http://foundationcenter.org/collections/
- The Gallup Polling Company, www.gallup.com
- The Pew Research Center, www.people-press.org
- Public Agenda, www.publicagenda.org
- Research International, www.riusa.com
- The Roper Center for Public Opinion Research, www.ropercenter.uconn.edu
- TNS Intersearch, www.tns-global.com

As you are refining your lists, keep in mind that you are seeking to identify people and organizations who are (a) linked or connected to you and your cause in some way, (b) have the ability to make a significant contribution and (c) have an interest in your cause.

This means that you no longer have to ask everyone you meet, but rather explore their interests and their passions. This results in a more relational, and enjoyable, experience for everyone involved.

Key Points

- By identifying who you're talking to, you'll be better able to target your communications.
- Look for linkage, ability and interest as you're identifying potential donors.
- Try to identify segments among your donors so that you can communicate more personally

FIVE: Awareness

In a difficult economic time, it's more important than ever to raise awareness and introduce more people to your cause. The primary reason: If people don't know about the need of the community and your organization, they won't become involved (or give). As Dan Pallota said in the Harvard Business Review, "spending money to build demand for the great causes of our time is as central to those causes as direct service — maybe more central, as it is the only way nonprofits have any hope of reaching the scale of the problems they confront".

The traditional marketing funnel aims to move people from Awareness through Consideration and Preference to Action and Loyalty. Nonprofit communication also aims for action and loyalty. If someone is aware that there is a need, they can consider various ways to address that need (whether through existing organizations or on their own). They select their preference and then take action (volunteering, donating or engaging in some other work). Ideally, they will become advocates for the organization and increase their involvement (perhaps by encouraging others to become involved with the organization or through a planned gift).

When marketing a nonprofit organization there are two messages that need to be communicated. First, educate the community about the need (to increase awareness). If potential advocates do not know that there is a problem, they won't become engaged in it. Next, build credibility of the organization (to increase the possibility of your organization being selected as the way to address the community need). You'll want to make the case that your organization is the best one suited to address those challenges.

There are ways to invest in marketing and communications without spending a lot of money. Creativity can go a long way in gaining attention from the media. Katya Andresen shares in her blog about a nonprofit in Seattle that adopted a chicken (trying to cross the road) as a way to build awareness of the need to be a more 'walkable' community.

We live in a very generous society and people want to support those causes they are engaged in and passionate about. By raising awareness and inviting people to engage in the organization, you will be one step closer to fulfilling your mission.

Nonprofit Marketing Trends

Before we jump into goals and strategies, I thought you might enjoy seeing some information about how other nonprofit organizations and using marketing techniques. The following statistics come from the 2011 Nonprofit Communications Trends Report.

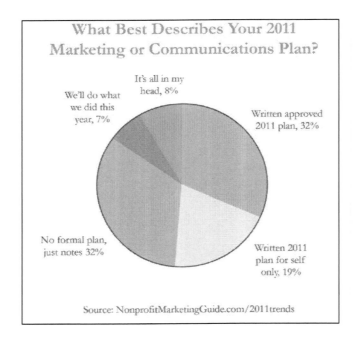

As you can see from this graphic, 51% of respondents had a written plan, but only 32% had it approved in some fashion.

Another question in this survey related to how important the organizations saw each of the following communication tools. This is probably the first year that Facebook outranked in-person events.

Communication Tool	% who ranked the tool Very Important or Somewhat Important
Website	96%
Email Marketing / Email Newsletters	94%
Facebook	79%
In-Person Events	67%
Print (Newsletters-Direct Mail)	67%
Media Relations / PR	57%
Twitter	34%
Blog	27%
Video (YouTube, etc.)	26%
Paid Advertising	21%
Phone Calls / Phone Banks	17%
Photo Sharing	11%
Audio (e.g. podcasts)	6%
Texting	4%

Source: 2011 Nonprofit Communications Trends Report, available at:
http://nonprofitmarketingguide.com/2011trends

Frequency of mailing and emailing is a topic that comes up fairly often. There are several nonprofit leaders I've talked to who resist sending more than quarterly contacts to their constituents. It doesn't seem that the respondents to this survey had any qualms regarding regular communications as 72% indicated that they emailed at least monthly.

Please Wipe My "Eyes"; (Or Things That Get Lost In Translation)

Several weeks ago I introduced you to my brother Frits. He always had great insights and was able to see the humorous side of things. For those new to my blog, Frits had muscular dystrophy, so was confined to a wheelchair for much of his life. He passed away in 2003. Here's a short story I loved to hear him tell (in Frits' words):

> A couple years ago (in 2001), I had a Hispanic nurse with a fairly heavy accent. It was morning, and as is often the case, I needed to wipe my eyes. So I asked Mildred (not her real name), "Will you please wipe my eyes?" So, she goes to the closet to get some tissue but she also comes back with a couple of gloves. I thought nothing of it because I figured some people would rather use a glove. But, then, she goes to start turning me over. Confused, I said again, and "I need to wipe my eyes," trying to emphasize my words very clearly so she could understand me better. Again, she starts to turn me over again. I say, no, I need to wipe my eyes. Then, all of a sudden she starts to laugh. She finally understood me. Amongst her laughing, she said to me that she thought I had said, "I need to wipe my a**." Very funny.

So much can be lost in translation.

When you describe what your organization does and the issues you address, what type of words are you using? Do you use a lot of acronyms? Buzz words that only those in your industry understand? Terms like recidivism, myocardial infarction, planned giving, etc.?

As you're putting together your materials, let someone who is not in your industry read it and give you feedback. Better yet, tell a fifth grader what you do – then write that down and use it instead. It doesn't mean talking down to your readers, simply making it easier for them to read.

Here's a bonus tip on your materials: always have a call to action. A call to action means one call to action (otherwise it get buried and then readers are not always sure what you want them to do). Deep down, I think everyone wants to help (yes you can call me naïve or too optimistic – I won't change my mind on this). So make it clear what you're looking for, make it easy to respond, and be sure to say thank you (often).

Tools

Jump starting your fundraising program means introducing your organization to people with the capacity to give large gifts. I just say that to remind you that, as you look at these strategies, you should consider whether or not they have the ability to put you in front of those potential major givers.

It would be very easy to spend a lot of time on any of these tools, so you'll want to target in on a maximum of three to five to start. This chapter is not designed to help you complete a full marketing plan, but it will provide some basics to help you get started.

These are some headings I've used in developing a brief table to keep track of awareness raising efforts:

- **Target markets** – who you will be communicating with
- **Goals** – what you want them to do
- **Strategies** – what you will do to encourage them to do that
- **Metrics** – how will you know that you've accomplished your goal?
- **Person Responsible**
- **Status** – converts the plan from something that sits on the shelf to something that will be shared at every board meeting (and/or staff meeting) and will be a dynamic, useful document

Crawl – Walk – Run

Don't feel like you need to do everything - you'd just get really overwhelmed. I've often heard people talk about the Crawl – Walk – Run philosophy. Basically, it acknowledges that we all need to start somewhere.

I'll be covering some of the 'main ideas' related to each tool. If you need additional help / support related to these, there are several how-to videos and support networks all over the web. Just type in 'how to twitter' or 'how to write a press release', etc.

Goals / Call To Action

As you select your strategies and begin to develop your plan, keep in mind that there should be a goal to each communication you send out. If possible, you'll want to track whether or not that goal was accomplished. So each piece should include a call to action of some sort. You could be trying to increase awareness, recruit more advocates of your organization, find new volunteers or increase donations. Whatever the goal, include an appropriate call to action and try to build in a way to measure the success of the campaign.

Website

Main Point?
The primary thing to remember in relation to your website is that it is the central point for all of your online activity. The majority of people who make gift online do so from the organization's website – and if their curiosity is piqued by your social media activities, they will find their way to your website. So – start here if you do not have a website already.

Financial Cost?
An ad supported website can be free (ie website tonight with GoDaddy). However I recommend that you pay for hosting (otherwise you have no control over the messages your visitors see). Depending on the size and the complexity of the site, you can pay anywhere from $50/100 per year to a few hundred dollars per month for hosting. I've seen complex websites that were $80,000 - $100,000, but most organizations have no need for that type of complexity.

Time Cost?
Whether you build it yourself or have someone to build it for you, content development takes time. Review what other successful websites do – and imitate it. If you're building it yourself, WordPress templates have made it easy to develop a website and make changes / updates (and you don't need to be too technically savvy). There are several free templates available for Wordpress.

Who will you reach?
Anyone with web access (but they need to be directed to the website somehow – print messages, e-newsletters, ads, search engines, etc.).

What format can the message take?
Very flexible using HTML, Flash, etc.

Best use?
To provide a general overview of the organization and provide opportunities for people to become engaged with the organization. You can also create unique landing pages for various appeals.

Email and Fundraising - Does it Make a Difference?

Have you been tempted to abandon your email strategy? Or avoid starting one in the first place? Convio released results from a study earlier this year that suggested that might be a bad idea.

They partnered with the ASPCA to test some different strategies. Those donors who received emails in addition to other communications gave more than those who did not receive emails. Here's what they found:

- Gave 112% more on and offline
- Gave 85% more gifts
- Saw a 54% increase in recency
- 15-20% higher average gift

But how do I get people to give me their email addresses? And what do I do with them once I get them?

Your first task is to identify what it is your donors / soon-to-be donors want. Talk to them – ask them. Then provide the information they are looking for and make it available in a regular email (and no, quarterly is not often enough).

While you're at it, take a look at your website too. Are you sharing stories? Is it about changing lives or simply an online brochure that lists what you do (Hint: people are generally more interested by stories and transformed lives).

Where do you get the email addresses? One starting point is to have a line on your reply device that allows people to enter their email address so that they can receive communications from you (but make it a compelling reason for them to give you that information). Another source is when you're speaking. Have a sign-up sheet to make it easy for people. And, don't forget to add a sign-up box to your website. Wherever you're interacting with people, make it compelling and make it easy.

The next step is to communicate regularly. If you wait too long between communications, people tend to forget that they signed up for the list. And guess what they do when that happens. Yep. You get marked as spam. Communicate regularly and with good information that they will find useful.

E-Mail Marketing / Newsletter

There are many resources available to help manage your email campaign. Some of the most popular ones include: Constant Contact, Vertical Response, and MailChimp.

Main Point?
One of the biggest challenges marketers face is building an opt-in email list. It's not recommended that you purchase email lists. Some other alternatives to building your list include:

- Adding a "signature line" at the end of each of your e-mails
- Collecting email addresses at public events
- Including a subscription opt-in on your website. As an incentive, offer a relevant, interesting report to people who subscribe.

Financial Cost?
Minimal (from zero to about $100 per month depending on the size of your email list). Using a management system for your email campaigns may cost a little, but the time you save in trying to manually keep a list updated is well worth it. A management system can help you track click-throughs, manage bounces, help you track what information people are responding to and adjusting future emails accordingly.

Time Cost?
This will change depending on your annual strategy. But it is possible to keep it really simple. A monthly two-three paragraph update might be sufficient.

Who will you reach?
Anyone who shares their email address with you. Let me restate the importance of not purchasing email addresses. First, most of the reputable email management companies will not let you upload a purchased list. Secondly, once you get flagged as spam it's really difficult to get off the list. Lastly, sending unsolicited email is simply bad form.

What format can the message take?
Just about any – from a simple letter to a full blown designed email

Best use?
Very flexible. Can simply convey information, including polls, links to surveys, etc.

Print

Main points?
With mail, it can be easy to get lost in the pile. Keep it simple, direct, and make it easy for someone to make a gift or get involved. Costs can add up, so make sure you're sending to the right list

Financial Cost?
Can get expensive. Need to keep in mind:
- Content creation
- Design
- Mailing lists
- Printing
- Processing (if you use a mail house)
- Postage – you can save money by mailing by mailing at the nonprofit rate, but allow plenty of time for mailing as it goes out at the convenience of the post office. Also, make sure you adhere to post office guidelines regarding weight, size, etc. as irregular pieces can increase the price significantly.

Time Cost?
Planning the campaign, creating content, printing, sorting. Some of this time can be saved by using a mail house.

Who will you reach?
Anyone you have a mailing address for.

What format can the message take?
Fairly flexible. If possible, integrate with an online campaign to increase the possibility of a positive response.

Best use?
Reaching a new group of people you are not currently interacting with. Also staying in touch with current supporters and augmenting online campaigns.

In-Person Events

Main Points?
Be clear on your purpose for having the event. It could be:
- Get to know us? (then to what end?)
- Raise Money?
- Recruit advocates?

Financial Cost?
Events can be expensive, but there are opportunities to get things donated as well.

Time Cost?
Can be very time consuming. Ideally you'll have a volunteer committee to run it with staff to serve as liaison with the organization (NOT to do all the work). If staff is heavily involved, make sure you're tracking their time to get a clear picture of the full cost of the event.

Who will you reach?
People who like to attend events. There was a study several years ago entitled 7 Faces of Philanthropy. One of the Faces was the Socialite who loves attending events. Terry Axelrod coined the phrase 'Point of Entry' events to describe get to know us events. You can read more about that in the Benevon / Raising More Money books.

What format can the message take?
Flexible. But make sure the organization is clearly represented in the event so that it becomes the first step of involvement, rather than just a fun event they attended.

Best use?
Raising awareness with a group of people likely to support or advocate for your cause.

Also, you can plan a targeted event – something special and unique that only you could provide – to a very selective group of people with the potential to give a major gift to your organization as a way to begin to engage them in your work.

Twitter: Productive Tool or Waste of Time?

I think the jury's still out on this one. A handful of organizations have had great success with fundraising, but the majority have yet to see tangible results.

But just because something is not directly related to immediate dollars doesn't mean that there isn't a long-term financial impact. A few years ago I was serving as the statewide development director for an international organization. In an effort to connect with our donors (some for the very first time), we asked some of our board members to host gatherings in different locations around the state. Our contributors loved it. In some cases, this was the first direct interaction they had with anyone related to the charity. And there was no money raised.

But... over the next six months, gifts by people who had attended these gatherings contributed a total of 70% more than they had given the prior year. A success? I think so.

Any tool that helps us build a closer relationship with our donors can have a long term impact. So instead of asking whether Twitter is a waste of time, maybe we should redefine what we're expecting.

Social Media: Facebook / Twitter / LinkedIn / Google+

Main Point?
Great way to stay busy for hours. Can be a good way to get a quick pulse of what people are talking about. Spend some time listening before you jump in. With the extensive growth social media is experiencing, it has proven that it is not just another fad, but the best use is still emerging. Watch and see what other nonprofits are doing and gauge whether you have either a large enough following – or the right online leaders as part of your group – to make this work for you.

Financial Cost?
Zero. Although there are some paid advertising options on some platforms.

Time Cost?
Can be extensive – with absolutely zero return. Be sure you know your goals ahead of time.

Who will you reach?
Anyone who is active on that particular platform.

What format can the message take?
Updates, messages to your members, longer messages, polls, surveys and other interactive formats. Twitter is limited to 140 characters – no graphics, although there are some tools that will allow you to send pictures and send longer tweets.

Best use?
By creating a community, and by connecting your supporters to each other, you are building an engaged group of potential advocates and potential donors. Facebook in and of itself is not a fundraising strategy, rather an engagement strategy that can lead to donations.

Three Tips: Raising Awareness for Your Nonprofit

This past year, one of my clients recently had a front page article in the newspaper about them. The board chair attributes this directly to a fundraising / awareness plan I put together for them last year.

One of the suggestions in my report was to hold a community event to try and build partnerships with community members and other organizations serving the same population. The plan included sending press releases out. In response to that, the local paper sent out a reporter who wrote an enlightening story that highlighted one of their clients. The day after the article ran, the editor included a positive comment on the editorial page about them. You can't buy that kind of awareness and credibility. And even if you could, most small organizations wouldn't be able to afford it anyway.

So why did it work? And what are some tips to help you get this kind of awareness too?

- o   The press release was about something timely and newsworthy
- o   The agency had spent time finding and coaching clients who could speak about their first-hand experiences with the organization
- o   They didn't keep it to themselves

Don't be afraid of getting out there in a big way. You're doing great work and people want to hear about it!

Media Relations / PR

Main Point?
Media relations is a much more traditional mode of communications.

Financial Cost?
Minimal – unless you use the work of a PR agency or hire a PR professional at your organization.

Time Cost?
Need to spend time getting to know newspaper editors and writers. They are stretched thin, so if you can make their job easier by providing answers to their questions, you'll likely be seen as a good resource, rather than someone who just wants to get their name in the paper.

Who will you reach?
Anyone who reads the paper.

What format can the message take?
You will have little to no control over what is printed – warning – nothing said to a journalist is really 'off the record.'

Best use?
Raising awareness.

Blogging

Main Point?
Will you be sharing information useful for the reader, or do you just want to talk about yourself? (HINT: it's about the reader.)

Financial Cost?
Free hosting available, but it should be integrated in to your current site to make it easier for people to find it.

Time Cost?
Intense – however with practice writing gets easier. You will want to take it seriously. Having a blog and not updating it looks a little like the store that has a sign up but nothing inside any more.

Who will you reach?
People who read blogs (or who visit your website). People who read blogs might be likely to be blogging themselves, so if you're sharing good content, they can help you extend your reach.

What format can the message take?
Flexible – can compile existing content or develop new content. Can also share graphs and all types of other information.

Best use?
Define what it is you're hoping to get from the medium, then work towards that goal. If you're not a writer, recruit someone who is – or who can help you improve your writing.

Video

Main Point?
Video is a very powerful to send clear message about what your organization does and who it does it for. Remember the video we watched earlier in this program from Charity:Water? It's a great way to share your story.

Financial Cost?
It can be expensive to have videos created professionally (although not nearly as expensive as it used to be). Recording devices have gotten better and editing software isn't that expensive. It's also fairly simple to create a recorded presentation in Powerpoint and convert it to Flash. A simple video can still be powerful.

Time Cost?
Time intensive. Will need to outline what you hope to accomplish, write a script, record and edit. You may also choose to hire someone to help with this.

Who will you reach?
Can reach anyone with access to a computer by sending out an email link. It's not likely that someone would stumble on your video on YouTube, watch it and then send in a donation, so you'll need to determine ways to drive people to watch the videos. Some of them may choose to share it with their friends.

What format can the message take?
Very flexible – simple to complex.

Best use?
To augment and clarify your message. In some cases, videos can go viral and increase awareness about your organization quickly. However, it's next to impossible to know which videos will create that kind of energy.

Paid Advertising

Main Point?
This is a message you have complete control of.

Financial Cost?
Can get really expensive.

Time Cost?
It pays to hire someone who is an expert at ad creation.

Who will you reach?
Anyone who reads the publication or site (Facebook and other websites also offer paid advertising)

What format can the message take?
Can lay it out any way you want.

Best use?
To reach a specific group of people you know will be interested in what you're doing, if you can find the right publication / site to advertise on.

Phone Calls / Phone Banks

Main Point?
Works great if you have a built-in group of volunteers.

Financial Cost?
Depends on whether you're using volunteers or a paid company. Need to remember that it's a long-term investment if you're using paid solicitors. Generally first year costs will exceed income generated.

Time Cost?
Regardless if you're using volunteers or paid staff, will need to prepare scripts.

Who will you reach?
Anyone you have a phone number for.

What format can the message take?
Can write script – will need to be able to be learned quickly.

Best use?
If you have a volunteer team of callers or if you have a lot of money to invest in acquisition. Works great if used for stewardship rather than acquisition.

Closing Thoughts on Communication

Long-term supporters are the life-blood of successful fundraising programs. So why is it that we so often take our long-term supporters for granted? Think about it for a moment. How absurd would it be if we only called our parents when we wanted money? Or what if you only talked to your boss when you wanted a raise? How long do you think you would keep your job?

It's all about communication. I had a phrase that I used so often in college that my friends used to tease me about it. "Communication is the key" I'd say – whether it was a relationship question, job question etc. I guess I said it so often though because it was – and still is – true. I might clarify that a little further now by saying the effective communication is the key.

Communication is definitely the key when it comes to building long-term friends (i.e. supporters) for your organization. Here are three tips to think about as you are pulling together your communications plan:

Communicate Regularly. It might be tempting to try to cut back on messages that you send out. I know we're all overwhelmed with the amount of information we're processing each day. Our email boxes are overflowing, we have ads popping up all over the internet, we have RSS feeds that we're following, not to mention Twitter, LinkedIn and Facebook accounts to try and keep from running us over. It's tempting to cut back – to save other people from that information overload. Cutting back is not the answer. The real answer is to make your communications more meaningful. Make it something they look forward to receiving. Share stories about people your organization is helping. Make it meaningful.

Communicate Emotionally. This is where stories become so helpful. Instead of stating: 'this makes me angry,' share a story that would evoke anger. Let others come to their own conclusions about how they feel. When you read through your materials, pay special attention to assumptions that are made – instead, provide the backup that led you to that assumption so that the reader can make their own assumption as well.

Communicate Appropriately. There are so many possibilities for communication these days. The most important thing then is to find out where your people hang out and where they get their information. Then pick a few different ways to communicate and build an integrated message. This means (1) communicate where they are and (2) use different mediums to reinforce your message.

Key Points

- Select just three to five strategies to start with.
- Be strategic. Know who you're talking to and communicate appropriately.
- If you wait until everything is perfect you'll never get started. The most important thing is to take the first step.

SIX: The Ask

A few years ago when I started working with a new organization, they insisted that the largest gift we'd be able to get from an individual would be $300. When I asked why, they said it was the largest gift they'd received from an individual. Truth be told, it was the largest gift they'd asked for. A few months down the road, I asked one of the organizations leaders for a $5,000 gift. He not only said yes, but suggested that he would contribute an additional $5,000 to serve as his gift for the prior year. From $300 to $10,000. Would that help your organization?

As I've mentioned before, asking is not about begging. And it's not about selling. In major giving, it's about building a long-term partnership with someone who has resources and a passion for the cause your organization addresses.

Please notice – I did not say that they have a passion for your organization. And that's probably the biggest mistake most organizations make in their fundraising programs – they talk primarily about their organization – and many potential major donors are really turned off about that. We should be talking instead about (1) the cause, (2) the impact that your programs will make – that the donor will be helping to make happen and (3) about what the donor is hoping to accomplish with his or her gift.

In the chapter about identifying potential audiences, we talked about the importance of identifying people who are linked to the organization in some way, have the ability to give a gift and who have an interest. That means that by the time we ask for a gift, we should have already confirmed that the answer to each of these questions was yes.

When we talk about 'cultivation' in major gifts, it is partially about planting seeds about the organization and working up to asking for a gift. However, just as important in this process is discerning whether or not asking for a gift is appropriate at all. So the cultivation is primarily about seeking to find out if there is a linkage, ability and interest on the part of the potential donor to make a major gift.

Just Pick Up the Phone and Ask

A couple of years ago I was sitting in a committee meeting and we were discussing feedback we wanted from participants. We were coming up with all sorts of options using technology (and avoiding personal contact). But then I asked the question - how many people were we looking at? Was it 5,000? 500? 100? No - it was about 15.

With 5 people on the committee, and 3 phone calls each, we could get some great personal feedback with just a handful of calls. Plus it would help build a closer connection with our constituency.

While technology can support us in our fundraising and volunteer-building efforts, sometimes it can also be a crutch that enables us to put an artificial barrier between us and our donors (or volunteers or board members).

It is so easy to just send off an email - but a conversation with some open-ended questions can glean a lot of information. But, what do you ask? In case you need some thoughts, here are a few to help you get started:

- o How did you learn about our organization?
- o What made you want to get involved?
- o What is your favorite thing about our organization?
- o What is your least favorite thing?
- o What is it that you would most like to see us do in the next twelve months? (Don't ask this unless you plan on doing something with the information you gather.)

And please, if you're planning on asking for a major gift, whatever you do, ask in person, not by phone.

I think you'll be pleasantly surprised at how welcomed your call will be!

Managing the Cultivation Process

If you are working in an environment where there will be multiple people (volunteers, staff board members, etc.) building relationships with potential donors, it will be important to track these efforts. Most donor management software programs have the capacity to manage this process (sometimes referred to as Moves Management). Most people can handle up to about 200 donors manually. After that, it's essential to have a system to help you handle details so that nothing falls through the cracks. There are several affordable options available.

Prospect Profile

One form that is helpful is a Prospect Profile. This helps you keep track of those things that you learn through the discovery and research process of getting to know your prospective donor better. Or you may enter this data directly in to your donor database – if you have one.

A few things to keep in mind as you begin gathering this data:

1) Please don't write down anything that would be embarrassing for the donor.
2) Only track the information that is – or could be - relevant to your organization and asking for a gift.

If you will be doing a lot of prospect research, I strongly recommend that you refer to the Ethics Statement of the Association of Professional Researchers for Advancement. It's available at: www.aprahome.org .

Sample Prospect Profile

PERSONAL INFORMATION

NAME:		DATE OF BIRTH:
HOME ADDRESS:		CITY, STATE ZIP:
HOME #:	FAX #:	CELL#:
SPOUSE:	DOB:	ANNIVER-SARY:
CHILD:	DOB:	SPOUSE (City / State):
CHILD:	DOB:	SPOUSE (City / State):
CHILD:	DOB:	SPOUSE (City / State):

WORK INFORMATION

JOB TITLE:	SECRETARY:
OFFICE ADDRESS:	CITY, STATE ZIP:
OFFICE #:	FAX #: CELL#:
E-MAIL ADDRESS:	WEBSITE:

PERSONAL ACTIVITIES

EDUCATION:	
HOBBIES:	
FAITH COMMUNITY:	
CIVIC / VOLUNTEER:	
AWARDS / RECOGNITION:	
ACHIEVEMENTS:	
OTHER:	

POSSIBLE INTERESTS

LEADERSHIP:

GIVING:

VOLUNTEERING:

GIVING HISTORY

CURRENT YEAR:	SUPPORT TO OTHER ORGANIZATIONS:
PRIOR YEAR:	
2 PRIOR YEAR	

WEALTH INDICATORS:	
ESTIMATED NET WORTH?:	

INVOLVEMENT WITH ORGANIZATION

LINKAGE:

VOLUNTEERING:

PAST INTERACTIONS:

Cultivation Timeline

For each prospect, you will find it helpful to have a schedule or timeline for your visits. You will most likely NOT be asking for a gift on the first visit. This form will allow you to track that. Again, you might have a donor management system that helps you track this type of information. So in that case, you would most likely be entering your notes directly in to the system.

After each visit, you'll want to assess what you perceive to be the commitment to the organization, the potential gift level and the amount of cultivation that would be required. You also might determine that they are not a great prospect for a major gift. In that case, they will hopefully still consider making an annual gift.

Keep in mind that Pareto's 80/20 rule applies. 80% of the gifts you receive will come from 20% of the work. Unfortunately, it's next to impossible to predict ahead of time which 20% of work will have the most impact. Don't get discouraged if you're not getting results right away. Consistent effort over time will consistently provide results.

Sample Cultivation Timeline

ID / Status		Potential Gift Level		Agency Commitment	
A	Solicit	1	$25,000+	I	Superb Prospect
B	Some Cultivation	2	$10,000 – 24,999	II	Very Good
C	Extensive Cultivation	3	$5,000 – 9,999	III	Good
D	Stewardship	4	$2,500 – 4,999	IV	Fair
E	Qualify	5	$1,000 – 2,499	V	Poor

Name of Prospect: _____

Moves Manager: _____

Natural Partners: _____

_____

Codes: Status _____   Level _____   Commitment _____

Moves Plan:

1)   Date: _____ Activity: _____

Who involved: _____

Completed Date and Outcome: _____

Best Possible Outcome: _____

Minimum Acceptable Outcome: _____

2)   Date: _____ Activity: _____

Who involved: _____

Completed Date and Outcome: _____

Best Possible Outcome: _____

Minimum Acceptable Outcome: _____

Contact Reports

If you have multiple people making visits with potential donors, it's important to be able to track how things go. A Contact Report would be used by a volunteer or staff member to report back to the organization how things went. One item to be sure to include on the form is regarding what you're hoping to have come from the visit. It might be collecting a specific piece of information or it could indicate the level of gift you're hoping they will consider.

Just an aside on terminology – try to use informal terms – such as chat or visit – as opposed to more formal terms like meeting or appointment. I can't really explain it, but somehow that seems to take the edge off when you're scheduling time to visit with a potential donor.

SAMPLE CONTACT REPORT

Prospect Name: _____ ID #:_____

Contacted By: _____

Date of Contact: _____ Duration: _____

Type of Contact: ☐ letter ☐ phone call ☐ personal visit (check location below)

Contacted Prospect: ☐ at office ☐ at home ☐ at agency
☐ other _____

Purpose:

☐ Stewardship ☐ Discuss Estate Plans ☐ Thank You Visit
☐ Solicitation ☐ Cultivation

_____

_____

Best Possible Outcome: _____

_____

Least Acceptable Outcome: _____

_____

Plan: _____

_____

Comments: _____

_____

_____

_____   _____

Signature of person preparing report   Date

Engaging People in Your Work

Through the major gift development process, you are encouraging people who have the potential to give major gifts to become engaged with your organization. There are a small handful of people who might start out by giving a large gift, but the majority will want to find out more about the organization first.

You'll see that, on the list below, there are many options for getting involved. Most people will start near the bottom – ie visiting the web site and signing up for a newsletter and work their way up. A handful of people will become advocates for your organization and recruit friends and family to also become involved.

High Engagement
        Make a significant gift
        Recruit friends/family
        Upgrade monthly donation
        Signup for monthly giving
        Renew donation
        Make single donation
        Make a phone call on your behalf
        Write a letter on your behalf
        Attend an event
        Sign petition
        Share on Facebook
        Forward an email
        Subscribe to e-Newsletter
        Visit website
Low Engagement

Here are some other ideas to help you get started. Be creative though, don't just limit yourselves to these (or any other list of ways anyone else shares). Your organization is unique and therefore has unique ways to engage your donors. In that vein, some of these ideas won't work for you. That's okay - check out the rest that might work better in the context of what you do.

- Invite donors to share about something they're passionate about. It could be at a board meeting, at an open meeting or other forum (as appropriate).

- Keep in mind the topics that are of interest to your donors. If you come across an article that you think would interest them, send it out with a little note. We all like to hear that someone's been thinking of us.

- As appropriate, invite the donor to write about something they're interested about for your newsletter. It could also be an article about how their life has been transformed through their involvement with your organization.

- Draw on their expertise and invite them to sit on an advisory group, the board, or another committee.

- Periodically, invite one of your clients to send a note to the donor. It lets the donor know, in a very personal way, how much their support is making a difference.

- Ask for advice (but only if you really want the advice - if you're not planning on using the information, this would have the opposite effect and drive people away).

- Send out cards to help the donor celebrate birthdays, anniversaries, holidays, etc.

Methods to Ask

Here are some methods you might use to ask. In major gifts, you'll be relying very heavily on the person-to-person ask. Annual gifts are generally received from other approaches – such as phone calls, letters and emails or internet appeals.

While renewal mailings typically see about a 10% renewal rate, initial acquisition mailings are considered highly successful if they receive a 2% response. Between ½ and 1 percent is a typical response rate for and acquisition mailing.

- Person-to-person: 50% say yes
- Personal phone call: 20-25%
- Personal letter: 10-20%
- Phonathon: 15% (renewals)
- Fundraising event: varies
- Impersonal letter: 10% (renewals)
- Internet-based appeals (acquisition): .5-1%

Percentages from "Grassroots Fundraising Strategy Chart" published in Jan/Feb 2011 issue of *Grassroots Fundraising Journal*

A Simplified Four-Step Model

Here is a simplified four-step model to asking for a gift. It boils down to introduce, involve, invite and repeat. This will typically take place over a series of visits.

Introduce

First, you'll introduce your potential donor to your organization. This might be by running in to them at a community event, inviting them to tour your organization, or inviting them to take part in a special activity designed for them or to participate in an activity for your constituency.

If you're calling to make an initial appointment, you can say "I promise I won't ask for a gift at this visit." It clears up the air that (1) you're wanting to be respectful and get to know them – and let them know the organization – before jumping to that stage and (2) it makes it clear that an ask is in the future. This was a tip I picked up from Jerry Panas at one of his trainings several years ago.

In this phase, it's important to not jump ahead. Take time to find out more about them, what they enjoy, if they have a personal connection to your cause, and who they are as a person. At this point, it's not about them making a gift. It's about you being genuinely interested in them.

Arm twisting and guilt at this stage could result in one gift – but it certainly wouldn't leave a good taste in anyone's mouth. What you will be doing is determining whether or not to move ahead to the next stage and, if so, developing an individualized plan of how to proceed.

Involve

Next, if appropriate, you'll want to help them become engaged with your organization in some way – in a way that is rewarding for them. How you involve them will in many ways rely on what you learned about them in the Introduce stage.

For some people, it might be important to do something together as a family. For others it might be participating in a committee that relates to what they want to do professionally (or to something they want to learn more about). How you're involving them will be very individualized based on what THEIR needs and desires are.

In some cases, potential donors may only want to be involved through their giving, so you'll want to be prepared for that option as well.

Invite

After you've respectfully introduced them to the organization and involved them in a way that meets the prospective donor's needs, then you can start to think about the gift. By doing research and asking questions during the Introduce and Involve stage, you've gotten a good idea of how much they might contribute and how interested they are in your cause.

You'll want to ask for a specific amount to help minimize discomfort on the part of the donor. The donor uncomfortable? Yes you heard that right. A potential donor has no idea what is expected or needed. They're afraid that if they suggest too low that they'll be considered stingy. But if they go too high they might be frivolous.

An alternative would be to provide a gift range chart with recognition levels and ask them where they see themselves on the chart. But really, the best thing is to ask for a specific amount.

Repeat

Now, repeat. Except the introduce stage becomes cultivation – letting the donor know how their gift is being used. And continuing to show that you're interested in them as a person. This might sound harsh, but, if all you're interested in is the money, please find a different line of work.

Over the years I've had the privilege of meeting and working with some truly amazing people who are committed to helping improve their community. You'll find yourself blessed by spending time and getting to know philanthropists.

Overview of Asking for a Gift

Asking for a gift is something that many people find frightening. Most of this though is due to a misperception of what asking is all about. Please remember, asking for a gift is not begging. It's much more about inviting people to become engaged in your cause.

After you've asked a few times, you'll realize that, most times, the donor is really excited about the opportunity to get involved and help a cause. They have funding and a passion, and you have the program that can impact lives. It's a perfect match!

Know also that there have been whole books and multi-day seminars just about asking. So what I'm providing here is a simplified overview.

Step One: Preparation

Know Your Prospect. I've mentioned this earlier, but you'll want to make sure that you know your prospect. This includes the project they're most interested in and about how much they might be wanting to contribute.

Alternate Project / Amount. You'll also want to have an alternative ready in case you misread the signs during your research and initial appointments.

Methods of Payment. You'll want to know the methods of payment that can be made – ie by credit card, installments over time, through a donation of stock, etc. As an organization you'll decide ahead of time what the accepted forms of payment are.

Don't Go Alone. It is best to go out in pairs – this allows you to get feedback from two perspectives following the meeting – you'll be amazed at the number of times you'll hear different things.

Be Prepared. Be sure you have review the approach and roles for each person ahead of time so that you look organized. Also, be prepared to answer questions that might come up about the project, organization, or any other frequently asked question your organization might get.

Step Two: Initial Contact

During your initial meeting, you will NOT be asking for a gift. As well, during your initial conversation – by phone or at the grocery store, etc. will also NOT be asking for a gift.

Arrange a personal meeting at a private location. You'll want a private environment for this visit where you won't be continually interrupted. At the prospects home or office is ideal. If the prospect is married or other people are involved in the charitable giving, you'll want to talk with all parties involved.

Don't try to explain everything ahead of time. Don't mail any materials prior to the meeting. In fact, you probably won't be sharing campaign materials at all the first meeting. You'll probably want to bring some information about your organization.

Here's a sample script that you might use during your initial call:

> *"As you may know, I serve on the board of XYZ Organization. We are realizing that we need to do a better job of telling our story to the community. I would love the opportunity to meet with you to share with you the work that we are doing. Would Thursday or Friday afternoon work best for you?"*

An alternative to saying that you'd like to share more about what you do to saying that you'd love to get their advice (but only if you're really interested in their advice – an insincere gesture of interest is worse than no gesture at all).

Plan for a one hour visit. You'll want to provide a couple of specific options for a meeting time – this helps keep it simple for the person you're meeting with. If neither options work for them, then at least you know that there's a sincere interest in your cause before proceeding to the next step. You'll want to show respect for your donor's time, so plan on keeping the visit to one hour.

Do not ask for a gift by phone. Annual gifts that are smaller in dollar value can be asked for through a phone-a-thon or by mail. Large gifts take more consideration on the part of the donor. Insisting on an in-person meeting will increase the likelihood of obtaining a gift and it communicates how important the project is to you, the organization, and the community.

Step Three: Initial Appointment

Have I said it enough yet? Asking for a gift is not begging – rather, it's presenting an opportunity for them to be involved with a cause they already believe in.

Be relaxed. It could be a moot point, because typically you wouldn't be asking for a gift at the first visit anyway. The first visit is to find out more about the person you are meeting with to determine whether or not your organization is a good fit for them – whether or not your organization will help the donor accomplish what they want to through their giving.

Don't be in a rush. So be yourself, don't rush (but do be respectful of the time frame you've provided – typically one hour), and listen.

Be a good listener. But, 'what do I talk about?' you might ask. A good idea is to start by thanking them for what they have done for your community. Try to find some points in common and ask lots of questions. If you know that they have a connection to your cause, ask about that. Then you can use that as a segue to talk about an aspect of your program that addresses that particular issue. Don't feel like you need to talk about everything. Although, chances are, the potential donor will ask that question. Just remember, this is a conversation, not a presentation.

Step Four: The Meeting (8 parts to a successful 'ask' visit)

While every visit will not fit this specific outline, it's a great starting place. You can prepare your case statement in this order so that it will provide the outline for the visit.

1. Introductions. First, is saying hello and a little small talk to transition in to the meeting. Was the prospects daughter in a swim meet recently? Ask how she did.

2. Setting the Stage. Next, you'll want to thank the prospect for taking time to visit with you and set the stage for the meeting by (1) emphasizing why it is an exciting time it is to be a part of the organization and (2) sharing about your involvement with the organization. If I haven't said it before, it's important that the person asking for the gift to have made their own gift first. Ideally

the asker will be a contemporary of the potential donor and have made a gift equivalent in amount to what is being asked.

3. About the Organization. Third is to talk about the organization's other successes and its history.

4. Needs / Case. Then transition into talking about the needs of the people you serve. This is a great place to share a story about how someone's life has been changed as a result of your work. Ideally, this would be a 'typical' story of someone who benefits from your organization – or at least typical of the program.

5. Campaign Introduction. Now you'll want to introduce the campaign that will help address challenges similar to those of the person in the 'typical' story that you shared. How much will it cost? How long will it take to accomplish?

6. Campaign Specifics. Next you'll talk specifically about the campaign. For example, so far, we've raised over $100,000 of the $500,000 needed with the help of community leaders such as…. (you'll want to include a few names if possible).

7. The Ask. Finally - the ask. You're heart is racing – your palms are getting a little sweaty. Perhaps you're starting to feel a little faint… We'll talk more about possible reactions and what your response might be. As I've mentioned before, you'll ideally be able to ask for a specific amount with suggested payment terms. For example, you might be asking for a five year commitment of $5,000 payable at $1,000 per year.

8. Thank / Closing. Next is to say thank you and close. This could be a thank you for their time or a thank you for their gift. Either way, be sincere. Make sure you have clear expectations about what the next step is – whether a follow-up visit or phone call or a letter summarizing the agreement to be sent.

Three Keys to Increasing Your Average Gift

During my trainings on 'Asking' I love to see the looks on people's faces as they realize that they, too, can ask for money. It's fun to watch expressions turn from skepticism to curiosity to incredulous to thoughtful to tentative confidence. Then fast-forward a few weeks or months down the road and the person who was the most skeptical is now the biggest advocate for the organization and excited about asking for money. Just thinking about those experiences brings a big grin to my face.

Here are three simple ways to increase your average gift.

Ask for a larger gift. Yes I know, that sounds too simple, but let me explain. A few years ago I was working with an organization whose largest individual gift was about $300. Why hadn't they ever gotten more? They hadn't asked for more. Within a few months I had asked for a $5,000 gift (and received $10,000) from one of the organization's leaders.

Talk about impact. So often, we talk about the organization - how great we are, all about the programs, how much it will cost, etc. But we don't spend much time talking about how Sue is now able to go to school because her asthma is now under control. Or about Tom who now has a job and is able to provide for his family. Or Ben who is no longer going to bed hungry. Talk about how people's lives are being changed - and not as much about you.

Think big. It's easy to talk about programs and the technical side of things. But can you reframe what you're doing? You're not 'providing counseling,' you're helping people lead fulfilling lives. Now, do you want to do that just for your clients? Or for your whole community? Are you 'providing food baskets' or are you ensuring that your clients aren't going hungry. And again, are you doing that just for your clients or do you want to ensure that no one goes to bed hungry? You don't need to accomplish it on your own. More and more organizations are partnering with other groups to help make a bigger impact on the whole community.

ASKING

Asking for a gift can raise anyone's heart rate a little. One of the most important things I can suggest is that you shouldn't be afraid of being turned down. This is about the donor and the organization. You're just the conduit.

As you proceed through the meeting, you should be summarizing how things are going and testing for closure. Perhaps as you're talking through the campaign, you emphasize that you're looking for a $50,000 donor for a particular building – look really closely to see if they blink or show any other outward sign. If they nod, that's a great indicator that you're on the right track.

Again, it is so important to ask for a specific amount for a specific program or campaign.

Potential Answers (and what they mean)

The person you're meeting with will have one of four responses. They might say no, not now, they might offer a lower amount, or they might say yes! Here's some more information about what that really means and what your response should be

No. So often, we hear no and immediately clam up and try to run out the door as quickly as possible with our tail between our legs. But – let me share a little secret with you – in this situation, often no does not really mean no. What does No mean? I hear you ask. Typically, it means not yet. So you'll need to ask some clarifying questions:

Is there something holding you back from making a gift? Is there a different program you might be more interested in? Is there anything we can do to change your mind?

Questions like these should help you determine what their no means. Sometimes it just means no, but, because you've done your research and confirmed in person that there is an interest and ability, it typically means that there is something else holding them back.

Be sure to debrief afterwards with the person who has joined you for the visit – sometimes they will have picked up on something you didn't.

See if they would like to meet again, thank them for time and do your best to leave the door open for further discussion.

Not Now. Not now is another response you'll hear. Again, try to ask clarifying, open-ended questions to determine what the objection might be and talk through how the organization might be able to address it.

- They might have two kids in college and need to wait until they graduate to think about making a gift. Make sure you stay in touch during the interim time.
- Perhaps they've just made a big investment in their business and need to hold off on making a big commitment – you could ask if it would help if you extended the payments over a few years.
- They could be concerned about fiscal stability of your organization or any other myriad of things. Find out what it is and then determine how you might be able to address the concern.

If it's simple to address, you could make an adjusted ask – restating the agreement that you and the prospective donor have made – and then be quiet and wait again.

A Lower Amount is Offered. I love to see people's faces when I say this, so I'm sorry I can't see yours. But sometimes, if someone offers a lower amount, the right thing to do is to turn it down.

What?!?! I hear you saying.

In a campaign, it's important to find your lead donors first. Large gifts set the stage for the rest of the campaign, so a lower gift could negatively impact the momentum of your campaign. You need to know the person really well before trying this approach, but you could re-emphasize the importance of the campaign and the recognition benefits for giving at the original ask level to see if they would consider. Or you could offer that the payment time be extended. If it's an issue of campaign momentum, you may suggest that you'll come back again at a later date – when the timing with the campaign is right.

Or, in some cases it's best to gratefully accept. That's part of the art of fundraising – knowing when to accept and when to suggest another visit at a later date.

Yes. When a donor says Yes. Say thank you, wrap up the conversation, and leave. Don't commit one of the major sins of fundraising and talk yourself out of a gift. It's been known to happen. Really.

Simply say thank you. Clarify the terms of the gift. And then leave.

And congratulations on getting that big gift.

Step Five: Follow-up (Stewardship)

As I've alluded to a few times, stewardship is a very essential part of the donor giving cycle. Too often organizations are only in contact with a donor when they ask for a gift. Consistent contact will help to ensure that donors don't feel like they're being treated like ATMs.

Here are some thoughts on ways you can do that. Of course send the official acknowledgement letter, but also send a handwritten note. Throughout the year you'll want to stay in touch. Do you know when their birthday is? Send a birthday card. Did you see a picture of their daughter in the paper? Send a congratulatory note.

Are they supporting a particular project (or have an interest in a particular project)? Send regular updates.

Equipping Your Volunteers

I strongly recommend that you download this pamphlet and make it available to your board members. How to Succeed in Fundraising by REALLY Trying is a pamphlet written by former businessman turned philanthropist, Lewis Cullman. It is a great resource to provide to volunteers who may be asking for gifts on your behalf.

This free resource is available at www.lewiscullman.com. It is based on years of experience raising money as well as being asked for it. The booklet is a handy guide for anyone asking for money for a charitable cause.

EXERCISE: Practice Asking

I encourage you to practice asking. Call a friend and schedule some time (in-person) to practice. Or, better yet, schedule some time at your next board meeting so that all of your board members can ask each other.

At your next board meeting, split into groups of three. One person will ask, one person will be the potential donor, and the third person will be the observer and will provide constructive feedback.

Key Points

- Focus on the needs and desires of the potential donor – NOT your organization.
- Engage people in the work of your organization in the manner your donor / potential donor wants to be involved.
- An in-person ask is the most effective way to ask for a gift.
- Introduce, involve, invite, repeat.
- 'No' often means 'I'm not comfortable saying yes yet.'

SEVEN: Your Fundraising Plan

In this chapter, we'll be pulling everything together to draft a fundraising plan for your organization. This will be your road map to success and will help you focus on those strategies that will best help you reach your goals.

We'll be reviewing the four-step approach to asking for gifts and cover strategies to keep your donors. You'll determine how many potential donors you'll need – and at what gift levels. Then we'll cover strategies to include in your plan. And, finally, you'll pull your plan together.

As a reminder, here is an individual giving pyramid.

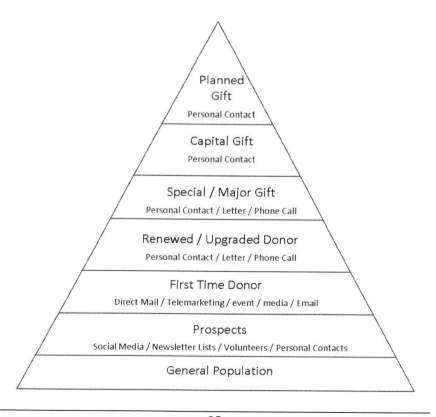

A fully developed fundraising plan would include strategies targeted at each level. Special and Major Gifts are typically asked for in-person and with individualized plans.

Prospects and the general population, unless they have the potential and interest to give a large gift would typically be approached by mail, through social media, or perhaps on the phone.

Review of A Simplified Four-Step Model

In the asking section, we talked a bit about the process of asking. In the major gifts context, this includes introducing the potential giver to your organization, involving them in a way they wish to be involved, inviting them (at the appropriate time) to contribute financially to the organization, and then repeating the process (not forgetting to say thank you multiple ways for the gift – seven is a great number to aim for).

Donor Retention

Several years ago, I heard of a group that was starting a homeless shelter for street kids in Central America. Many of these children were raising themselves on the street. The organizers were convinced that if they were able to get the children in the shelter, that they would be able to serve them. Unfortunately, this was not the case. The children would come, get some food, and then leave again through the back door. This seems to also be the case for many fundraising programs. A donor comes in once, but then doesn't see a need to stick around. By the way, the agency mentioned above was able to change their approach and impact the lives of many children.

The 2010 Fundraising Effectiveness Project found that for every 5.4 new donors recruited, slightly more than 6 donors were lost through attrition. No matter how good a job we're doing at getting new donors, if we can't keep the ones we have, we're going to be in trouble. The 2011 numbers did show an improvement, however the result was still a net loss.

In your plan, be sure to include a section on stewardship of current donors. You'll want to include several ways to help them stay informed about what your organization is up to between asking for a gift.

Why Donors Lapse

Adrian Sargeant completed this study on why donors lapse in 1999, but the information is still helpful for planning. There are a few issues that the organization would have no control over. However, if you look through this list, you'll see several of the issues are related to communication – 36.2% felt that other causes were more deserving – that tells me that organization wasn't doing a good job of communicating its' importance. The needs section of your case statement should provide information that proves how worthy your cause is.

18.4 % said they didn't remember supporting the cause in the first place. This might relate to attendance at an event where the cause was not at the center of the event. That's a great opportunity for most events.

13.2% said that the organization didn't acknowledge their support. An additional 8.1% said they weren't informed of how their gift was used and another 5.6% said that the organization didn't need their gifts anymore.

Each of these are opportunities you can address in your stewardship plan.

REASON	%
I can no longer afford to offer my support	54.0
I feel that other causes are more deserving	36.2
Death/Relocation	16.0
No memory of ever supporting	18.4
X did not acknowledge my support	13.2
X did not inform my how my money had been used	8.1
X no longer needs my support	5.6
The quality of support provided by X was poor	5.1
X asked for inappropriate sums	4.3

I found X's communications inappropriate	3.8
X did not take account of my wishes	2.6
Staff at X were unhelpful	2.1

Study by Adrian Sargeant, 1999. Available at: *www.nationalcne.org*. *Direct link: http://bit.ly/9Ovze6*

Growing Loyal Donors

Another study by Penelope Burke (*Donor-Centered Fundraising, Cygnus Applied Research, 2003*) found similar results. 93 percent of donors indicated that they felt these three communications issues were most important in determining long-term loyalty and lifetime gift value of the donor:

- Prompt and personalized gift acknowledgement
- Confirmation that funds will be used as originally indicated in the solicitation
- Measurable results on donors' last gift before they are asked for another one

Lifetime gift value is a great way to look at potential donor acquisition strategies. Often, the cost of donor acquisition will be close to, if not higher than, the actual gift amount. But if that person stays a donor, each additional gift has a much lower cost, resulting in a more solid program over time. So, it could be worth it to lose money on the first gift – if you know that you'll be able to encourage them to become part of your organizational family over a long-term period. They become partners and family rather than simply donors.

Motivations for Charitable Giving

This is just a list of some motivations donor reported related to making charitable gifts. But remember, surveys often report how people wish they were, rather than how they are. However, these are still good guidelines to use as you develop your communications.

Reported Motivations for Charitable Giving

Motivations	% of Respondents
Basic needs	43.0
Poor help themselves	36.7
Make community better	36.7
Make world better	35.4
For equity (responsibility to help those with less)	27.9
Own decision about money	25.3
Services government can't/won't	23.4
Solve problems in world	17.5
Same opportunity	16.4
Support friends and family	13.8
Diversity	6.0
Ties across communities	4.6
Other	2.3

Source: The Center on Philanthropy at Indiana University using data from Knowledge Networks.

5 Steps to Retain Donors

There are five steps you can take to ensure donor retention that most experts agree on. These are loosely based on an article in Advancing Philanthropy (on page 28-29 in the May/June 2010 issue).

1. First, know your donor. Do research, find out what they like and appreciate, ask them. Then recognize them and ask for support in an appropriate manner based on what you've learned.
2. Second, be donor-centered, rather than organizationally centered. Donors have goals that they are trying to reach with their giving. Help them reach their goals.

3. Communication is the key – communicate regularly between asking for a gift to ensure the donor feels appreciated and knows how their prior gift is being used.
4. Show appreciation on a regular and ongoing basis.
5. And finally, identify outcomes – and share what the impact of your programs are – and how lives are being changed – as a result of the donors support.

Obtaining Feedback From Your Supporters

A great way to prepare for a campaign (whether an annual campaign or major gift campaign) is to do a survey with your current constituents. This can provide great information – such as what people think of your organization, what things they think you might do better, if they might consider giving (or giving more) to your organization, what is important to them, etc. But, how do you create a survey that people will actually take the time to complete? Here are five things to think about.

First, how are you distributing the survey? It needs to be easy to complete the survey and get back to you. There are some great on-line tools that can assist with that. Zoomerang and SurveyMonkey both have free options for small surveys. It should be sent with a brief introduction that outlines how long it will take to complete. It should also include an overview of how the information will be used. A stand-alone invitation should be sent.

Next, how long is your survey? If it's too long, people will not be willing to take the time to answer it. If it's not long enough, you won't get the information you need. So it is very important to define what you most want to get from the survey and not ask questions that won't be relevant for your purpose.

Is it well-written and does it work? Poor grammar, misspelling words and run on sentences can easily turn responders off. In on-line surveys, plan on having a small group test the survey to make sure that everything works properly before it is sent to the full list. I recently went on-line to complete a feasibility study survey for a charity that my husband and I support. The survey didn't work properly and we were unable to complete it online.

Finally, does the format make sense? Typically if you are asking someone to rank how they feel about something, it's best to have an odd number of options (if they don't feel one way or the other about, they can select the neutral (middle) option. With questions that have multiple choices, you'll want to include an 'other' selection.

Offering some type of incentive for participation can also help. Maybe a free registration to an event that you would typically charge for, or a gift certificate from a local restaurant (in many cases you may be able to get one donated – it would provide visibility for the restaurant). There are many options, but try to find one that relates to your organization.

Your Plan

By pulling together everything in a central document, you'll be able to have a better idea of the full picture of everything you're working on. In some cases, you may realize that you are trying to do too much. If that's the case, spend some time going through your projects and prioritizing. Perhaps there's a project that just needs to be put on hold for the time being. Don't get rid of it completely, just change the anticipated date to be completed to six months, a year, or two years out. Then you'll be able to get back to it at a better time.

Your plan will include overall goals, objectives, activities, notes about the status, and the person responsible. You might also want to use your plan as an agenda for meetings – then it can be a dynamic document that is continually being referenced, updated and shared.

The rest of this chapter, I'll be walking you through a step-by-step process to set your goals, segment your donors, and determine the right strategies to use.

Setting Goals

A Gift Range Chart is a great tool to help you determine how many donors – and prospects you will need to reach your goals. Once you've completed your chart, you may realize that you don't have enough prospects. That's okay – that information will provide you will a goal.

You'll be focusing your time on the top four rows of the chart below. If your total goal is $100,000, this chart might work for you.

You'll notice that the largest gift is 10% of the total goal. All told, 30% of your donors will typically account for about 80% of the total amount raised.

ABC Organization

FY 2011 Sustaining Campaign

Gift Range Chart

Gift Range [A]	# of Gifts [B]	# of Prospects Needed Per Gift [C]	# of Prospects [B*C]	Cumulative Prospects	Total per Range [A*B]	Cumulative Amount Raised	
$ 5,000	2	5	10	10	$ 10,000	$ 10,000	10% of donors / 60% of goal
$ 2,500	6		30	40	$ 15,000	$ 25,000	
$ 1,000	18	4	72	112	$ 18,000	$ 43,000	
$ 500	34		136	248	$ 17,000	$ 60,000	
$ 250	48	3	144	392	$ 12,000	$ 72,000	20% of donors / 20% of goal
$ 100	80		240	632	$ 8,000	$ 80,000	
under $100	412	2	824	1456	$ 20,000	$ 100,000	70% of donors / 20% of goal
	600		1456		TOTAL:	$ 100,000	

Setting Goals: Non-Cash Measurements

This may surprise you, but just because you raise more money this year than last year does not mean you have a healthy fundraising program. Here are some alternate indicators that are good to keep track of:

- Donor Retention
- Engagement

- Median Gift Size
- Non-Ask Contacts
- New Donors

Segmenting Your Audiences

Now you'll want going to segment your donors. Something to keep in mind is that in major gifts, each prospect could be their own 'segment.' For the donor group, you may include a group of people, or you might list individual names.

What are the identifying factors that distinguish them as a group? You'll want to know about how many people are in each group as well as what's important to them. It's also important to identify what it is about them that you still need to find out, things related to giving that you don't know yet. Take some time to think this through. It will help you determine which strategies are appropriate to use with that particular group.

Determine Strategies

We're about to review some strategies. Many of these may sound familiar, as we covered a lot of this material in the chapter on awareness. Feel free to go back and review that information if you need, since that covered everything in a lot more detail.

For each of the items you included in your 'what we still need to know' list, determine the appropriate goals. Then you'll want to focus on the strategies that will best help you accomplish that goal.

The more engaged someone is with your organization, the higher likelihood that they will become long-term donors. If someone visits your website, are they invited to receive ongoing updates about your organization? Do they receive alerts when an activity will be going on in their region?

With your segments, it might help to identify how engaged they are, and then determine ways to invite them to become more involved. If someone has given a one-time gift, invite them to give on a monthly basis. You can ask your bank or other credit card vendors about how to set this up.

If they've given for several years, they are probably a good prospect for either a major gift or a planned gift (through their will or perhaps a gift annuity or charitable remainder trust. If you don't already have a planned giving expert on your board or involved in your organization, I highly recommend it.

Individual Approaches

Phone calls, mailing items of interest to the donor (related to the organization or not), emails and personal visits are just a few ways you can interact with your donors to build long-term relationships with them.

You can call to say thank you, write personal handwritten notes or a more formal letter. One organization I have given to (and continued to give to) had a board member call to say thank you. It didn't matter that it was my husband's and my first gift and the board member thanked us for being a long-term supporter, we were just honored that they called.

Mass Approaches

If you're trying to interact with a larger audience, personalization is key. If you don't have an easy way to do that, it's time to either learn how to do it on your current donor management system or, if your system doesn't have the capabilities, to upgrade to a new system that does. There are several affordable options available. Techsoup.org has some great resources to help you select the right database for your organization.

Appreciation events have been highly successful for organizations I've worked with. In one case, it resulted in a 50% increase in gift size among the attendee group.

Other ways are regular updates – either by email or mail, newsletter, using social media tools and taking advantage of press and media coverage. Webinars as a donor engagement tool are beginning to become more popular. Just make sure the information you are sharing is timely and relevant for the publication you're sending it to.

Metrics / Tracking

Over the past few years we've been hearing about various ways that not-for-profit groups should be evaluated. In the US, the conversation has been focused primarily on financial indicators of success (i.e. overhead rates that simply measure the percentage of total dollars that appear to go directly towards programs rather than to 'overhead' costs such as administration and fundraising). If you've ever tried to run a committee that doesn't have a leader or organizer you probably have an idea of how short-sighted this measurement is. So what do we track as an alternative? Some organizations are now rightfully attempting to present alternative ways of ranking nonprofits that go beyond financials, but in your everyday life of running a nonprofit organization, what evaluation outcomes should you be tracking in your fundraising program?

There are three primary reasons for starting/continuing an evaluations component for any program. Primarily, it gives you something to reach for. In Alice in Wonderland one of the characters points out that if you don't know where you are going, any road will get you there. Stephen Covey offers this as Habit 2 in his book The Seven Habits of Highly Effective People; that is to Begin with the End in Mind." In the nonprofit sector, we have funders who require it (along with the general public). And if we don't define what we want to measure ahead of time, it's likely that a funder or government body will come up with something that could be more difficult and expensive to track (and may be a less accurate measure of what you are attempting to accomplish). In addition, evaluation is important because it helps us see what's working (and what's not working). Just because a fundraising program works well down the street or for a similar agency in a different part of the country doesn't mean that it will work just as well for your organization. So evaluation will help you to determine what to continue (and what to discontinue) for your organization's fundraising program.

There are many things that you could track in your fundraising program. The one aspect that most people seem to want to jump to first is money. However I'm going to be so bold as to say that I believe that's the second (or even third) thing that should be measured. Short-term strategies to bring funding in the door quickly could be detrimental to the overall fundraising program and long-term donor intentions. By building long-term relationships with donors, we can ensure a longer-term commitment by the donor (resulting in higher lifetime giving from the donor). It's quite expensive to acquire a new donor, so the longer they feel an affinity to the organization the better. We want to measure revenue, but interim measurements (such as the numbers of contacts that are made to each donor/prospect, awareness, numbers of volunteers, etc.) may be more important. A third aspect to measure is the cost of fundraising (with a long-term perspective). Not all of the cultivation work that is done this year will result in a gift this year. In fact at one organization I worked at several years ago, it took a full six years or cultivation and negotiation to finalize a $7 million lead gift for a capital campaign. Patience does pay off. There are many smaller groups that don't have the ability to invest funds in the mean time, but it is an investment that will pay off.

There are many ways to track the indicators listed above, but your primary tool will be your donor database. There are many options out there, and most will provide what you need. However there is no one software program that will be the best choice for every organization. TechSoup.org offers some information to help in this selection process. It's important to assess what you need it to do, and then select the one that will meet your needs. In addition, be mindful of the GIGO principle (Garbage In, Garbage Out). Spending the time ahead of time to determine how your data will be tracked will be much easier than trying to adjust data once it has been entered inconsistently. A common challenge I've seen in this area is that software programs and database administrators often speak a different language than fundraising professionals. This communication breakdown can often leave the fundraising professional believing that the database can't do what they want it to, when in reality they may have asked something in a way the database administrator didn't understand.

Keep it simple. We can spend hours creating plans and reports that give us lots of information, but nothing helpful in planning for the future or accurately evaluating what we've accomplished. Identify the 3-5 primarily things that really make a difference in your organization. Then focus on those. Also, test different mailing packages, test different strategies with different donors. You might have some gut feelings about different tactics, but very often our donors don't think the same way we do. Through testing, some of your gut feelings will be confirmed (and in some cases you may be surprised by the findings). And finally, you can do it. Don't be overwhelmed by everything that needs to be done, just pick the important things to focus on. You can do it. Really.

Here are a few things to track:

- Financial goals. Year-to-year, you can compare how much each strategy is costing you – and what the return is, your average gift size and whether it is increasing or decreasing.
- Participation goals. Including board giving and repeat givers.
- Interim measurements. Including the number of people who are asking, how many people are being asked, and the number of contacts.

Donor Management Systems

It's exciting to see how technology has expanded the ways that we are able to accomplish the basics of fundraising (building relationships and customizing our communications). We're able to track and more easily access information about interests (remember the days of 3x5 cards and a hole punch?). We're able to more easily create targeted messages and send it out to just the people who are interested in it.

But, lately I seem to be running in to more and more groups who are trying to run their systems from homegrown Access databases and Excel spreadsheets. There's so much more that a good donor management system can provide.

In case your board and senior staff is looking for justification to back up your request to upgrade to a 'real' donor management system, here are some thoughts regarding the two primary purposes of such a system:

- Define who the organization's leaders should meet with.
- Reinforce a thoughtful, disciplined approach to fundraising.

How do you decide who you will meet with personally and who will receive other types of correspondence? In order to use your donors gifts wisely, it's so important to segment your donors. Now it's possible to sift through raw data, sort it, and try to visually gauge your strongest givers over time. But it is very time consuming and the process leaves open the possibility for human error. Most donor management systems will allow you to group your donors based on certain criteria to ensure that people don't fall through the cracks.

Data also helps to support a thoughtful, disciplined approach to fundraising. All of the literature relating to direct mail emphasizes that we need to test different approaches to see what works best for our own donors. What works in an international membership association won't be the same as what works for a local ministry (and vice versa). Do you have a one page letter with lots of white space? Or a four-page letter? It depends - test! A good donor management system will allow you to enter the data and easily pull a report that lets you compare those different campaigns.

Technology, including e-mail and social media, have added a whole new range of possibilities (and a near infinite number of data points to track). In an ideal world, your email campaign and social media campaigns could all be tracked from the system, and software providers are beginning to make changes to allow that. The possibilities are exciting.

Now I know what you're going to ask next. So what donor management system should I chose? Should I switch? Well, that depends too.

Your first step is to do a complete analysis of what you want your system to be able to accomplish. TechSoup offers some great resources to help you do that. In addition, the Association of Fundraising Professionals (AFP) offers an annual listing of software providers with information on the features each of their products offer. There are many more than these, but here are a few of the features that I see as essential in any system that is supporting (or will at some point) a major gift effort:

- Prospect lists
- Solicitation schedules
- Activity reports for management and volunteers
- "Moves" management reports
- Enable relationship building
- Allow for segmentation of donors
- Support donor recognition activities

The second step is to pull together a list of 3-5 systems that offer what you need that are also in your price range (different providers charge based on different criteria – i.e. number of concurrent users vs. number of unique users vs. number of records, or some combination thereof). Once you sit through some demonstrations you might want to change some of your criteria.

Key Points

- Set Goals
- Segment Your Donors
- Identify Strategies
- Develop Plan
- Implement
- Continuously Measure and Adapt

To review, if you haven't already done it, you'll want to start by using the Gift Range Chart to help you determine how many donors you'll need at each gift level. Then you'll either segment your donors, or for potential major donors you'll fill out information for each individually. Once you've identified your goals for each of your segments, you'll identify the strategies that will help you accomplish those. Finally, you'll compile all of that information in to a central document. That's your plan.

Before you start to implement your plan, review it to determine whether or not you're being realistic about what can be accomplished. Don't be afraid to put two or three strategies on the back burner for the time being.

As you implement, keep your plans up to date and use it as a roadmap for success. You can have confidence that by following your plan, you will begin to see results soon. However I'll warn you also, that the biggest results typically come after about 18 – 24 months. So please don't get discouraged if you only see small successes. It's at about 18-24 months that things start getting easier. Instead of having to go out and find people, they'll start calling you. Instead of having to beg the paper to run your story, the journalist will call you to see what you think. Having been through this process with several organizations, I can assure you that it will happen.

EIGHT: Volunteer Engagement

So far, this book has covered the essentials of starting, or growing, your fundraising program. This has included everything from developing a strong vision to putting that into a case statement. We've talked about different ways of raising awareness among potential supporters and also talked about ways to engage them in our work.

But with all of that, one essential ingredient remains, the importance of including volunteers in the raising of money and engaging them in cultivation and asking.

In this chapter, we'll also talk about some ways to address roadblocks that may exist among your current board. While you can't expect things to change overnight, by implementing some of these strategies you'll begin to see increased engagement among your board fairly quickly.

Steps in Engaging Volunteers

If there's one thing that seems to come up again and again as I talk with Executive Directors and Development Directors, it's that board members don't want to be involved in fundraising. And in some cases, I can't blame them. They've been recruited because someone thought that they'd say yes - not because of any passion for the cause. They were assured that all they would have to do is show up at meetings. And we get what we ask for.

That leads us to this first suggestion: Set expectations while you are recruiting potential board members. We get what we settle for, so please, don't be afraid to talk about what you really want your board members to do while you are recruiting them. In many cases though, we've come in down the road a ways and are, for the time being, stuck with those people who were either 1) recruited under a different set of expectations, 2) thought that said expectations didn't apply to them or 3) have gotten used to the status quo of not being involved with fundraising. In this (much more common) situation, here are a few steps to take.

Start with one person (or two). If you wait until you have everyone on board, you'll be waiting a long time. Having a little momentum is better than spinning wheels in place.

Do everything you can to make that one person successful. I've seen the transition from reluctant participant to engaged advocate. The transition occurs for a variety of reasons. Most important, I think, is that they get to see for themselves what an honor and privilege it is to ask for money. And they see firsthand that most donors are not offended by then ask.

Have that advocate share their experiences. It's one thing to have a paid staff member or consultant talk about raising funds. It's a complete other for a board member to see one of their own - who was reluctant not so long ago - now being enthusiastic about asking for donations.

Lastly, talk about fundraising at every meeting. Dr. W. Edwards Deming taught us that we should expect what we inspect. Using a dashboard of some sort makes that easier because then you're sharing the same type of information at each meeting. And go beyond just talking about the money.

Here are some basics to help you get started.

- Provide a job description for each volunteer position
- Develop materials that volunteers can use and reference
- Identify prospects for the volunteer position
- Ask for involvement
- Begin meeting / develop goals
- Provide feedback / encouragement
- Lead by example

What to Include in the Job Description

There are two ways to structure your fundraising efforts. Ideally, asking for funds will become a responsibility of every board member. However, I recognize that this is not possible in all organizations. In that case, you might want to start a fundraising taskforce or fundraising committee to help you get started. Regardless of which avenue you take, you'll want to develop a job description so that expectations are clearly communicated up-front.

Here are some things that you will want to include in your job description:

- Develop and <u>implement</u> a program for soliciting support (this helps to make it very clear that asking for support is a central expectation of their duties as a member of the board – or of the fundraising committee).
- Ensure that the 'case for support' is strong (A strong case for support is essential to finding people who want to come alongside you to help the organization achieve its mission for a stronger community. This committee will also bring some great insight into improving the case for support).
- Develop and implement strategies to cultivate prospects.
- Share information about the needs of the population and how the organization is meeting those needs (Raising awareness is another key activity that will increase potential donations).
- Develop an expectation for financial contributions from Board Members and provide leadership by making their own gifts (Since it is very difficult to ask for a gift if you haven't made a gift yourself, make sure it's clear that making a personal gift is expected).
- Solicit funds by contacting potential contributors
- Length of time commitment expected (this might be one year, three years or five years).
- Maintain confidentiality of all donor records (High ethical standards are essential in the raising of money. At the very least, you want to ask that all members maintain confidentiality of all donor records. Ideally, you'll also review and adopt the Ethics guidelines developed by the Association of Fundraising Professionals and also, perhaps, The Donor Bill of Rights, both available at www.afp.net/ethics).

Materials for Your Volunteers

Next, you'll want to develop materials for taskforce members to use (this includes the case statement, pledge cards, Frequently Asked Questions, etc.). Here is a list of the items that you'll want to provide those who are serving with you:

Pledge Card. A pledge form or pledge card provides an easy way for someone to make a gift for your organization.

Brochure. A simple brochure or one-page flyer provides to basics about your organization.

Ways to Give. You'll want to set up easy ways for donors to support your organization. This could include a 'donate now' button on your website, the pledge form mentioned earlier, and a monthly giving option. A monthly giving option is great for organizations that are beginning to get focused on increasing funds for their organization – for instance, $25 monthly becomes a $300 annual gift. That adds up!

Case Statement. This provides great information for your board or committee and help them share the story of your organization.

Identify Prospects

Who do you want to serve on your committee or on your board? Identify prospects in the community who have both the ability to give at a high level, are well respected in your community and who are committed to your cause.

Asking People to Serve

Now you'll ask those prospects if they would like to join you. Just like with asking for a gift, we need to ask people to consider serving.

In the initial meeting with your prospective board or committee members, be sure to provide information about both the needs that necessitate your program operating – and about how your program addresses those needs. Try to share this in a concise way that can be easily duplicated. While it's tempting to show off everything you know, keep it simple so that people can easily envision themselves doing the same thing.

You'll provide the job description AND go through the expectations together – don't just hand it to them and expect them to read it later. They might – but they might not.

Ask if they would consider joining you in your effort to address the community needs you referenced early. Remember – this is not about you – so don't take it personally if this is not a cause that your prospect is feeling called to. And if they're not interested, a great follow-up question is whether or not they might know someone who would be passionate about your cause.

And finally, ask for a gift. Since you've already walked through the expectations with them – and the expectations include making a personal gift – this will not came as a surprise. Even if they say no to serving on the committee, they may still be open to making a contribution to help you get started.

Goal Setting

One of the first things you'll want to do when you start meeting as a group is to set your goals. In your planning, you probably already have an idea of what some of those goals are. But by allowing the committee to be a part of that process, you'll increase their ownership of the goals – and therefore their commitment to achieve them.

You can cover overall goals for your fundraising program, but most important to talk about is what the appropriate goals are for the committee or board that are directly related to the involvement and activities of those committee or board members.

In developing your goals, it can be helpful to review past performance. In addition, be sure that your goals are SMART – that is specific, measureable, attainable, realistic and timely.

Helping Your Board Help You

Have you ever struggled to engage your board in fundraising? If yours is like most of the groups I've worked with, your answer to that was probably something like "you mean there are organizations who don't struggle with that?"

There are two sides to this issue. First is the need of the organization – money is needed, and, in the field, we generally agree that fundraising is one of the core responsibilities of the board.

On the other side are our board members. They have (typically) not studied fundraising. It is an unknown. While they are experts in their own fields, fundraising can be intimidating. And too often, we don't define what we mean and what exactly we're asking when we say we want board members to become involved in fundraising. It continues to be this vague unknown.

The 2011 Cygnus Donor Survey confirms our generally accepted idea that donors will give more when asked by volunteer leadership. In addition:

- Board Giving: 52% of board members serving organizations with fundraising staff said it was required. This dropped to 27% for those on boards of organization with no staff fundraisers.
- Board participation in fundraising: One in three board members surveyed said participation in fundraising activities was required.
- Board fundraising evaluated: 18% of Boards represented in this survey evaluate their performance in fundraising.
- Board orientation :> 40% of respondents indicated that had an orientation program when they joined the board.
- Training in fundraising: 49% reported having access to training in fundraising.

What difference would it make in your organization if you offered a road map for your board members by clearly defined expectations (giving, participation in fundraising efforts and define what 'participation' means), and then provided training and guidance?

Ongoing Meetings

Volunteer Led. Your ongoing meetings should provide encouragement and keep up the momentum of your campaign. Ideally, these meetings will be led by a volunteer (who would ideally be supported and trained by a staff member). Why a volunteer? Because that volunteer is a peer of the rest of the committee. It's not the committee's job to come up with work for the staff person, but if the staff person is running the meeting, it can be difficult for them to communicate that to their committee or board. The volunteer leading the meeting can easily turn the meeting back to focus on what the committee or board is responsible for.

Moment for Mission. Try to include a moment for mission – this is most typically a story about someone who has been helped. It helps the group stay focused on the big picture – rather than get mired down in the details.

Provide Encouragement. As you meet, you'll want to provide ongoing support and encouragement. Be a cheerleader for your group – celebrating your small successes will help keep momentum going. Inviting a group member to share about their success is a great way to (1) show how easy it can be and (2) it also gets others excited about trying it themselves.

Provide Feedback and Training. Feedback and additional training is great to include as well. Find out what challenges people are having – then invite other group members to share their thoughts.

Lead by Example. We can't expect others to do what we won't. Leading by example also enables us to model those activities we want our board members to repeat and thereby help them better understand what is expected. In this vein, don't forget to lead by example.

Some Words of Caution

Before we proceed, here are a few words of caution.

First, we carry a lot of baggage about money. Spend some time analyzing your own feelings and what you've been taught about money. If you focus on the results of money raised, rather than the money itself, you might find asking for gifts easier.

Secondly, don't make up all the goals by yourself in a vacuum. Let your volunteers be part of the process – this increases ownership of the goals – increases their commitment to them – and greatly increases your chances of success.

And finally set clear expectations and guidelines. These make it easier for someone to decide whether or not they are able to fulfill those expectations. It also avoids the unfortunate circumstance when someone says, "but no one ever told me that!"

Overcoming Obstacles

Most of the obstacles we're going to address relate to trying to engage a board of directors who has never been expected to raise money. There could be many reasons for this, but we won't focus on the reasons here – just some ways to turn it around.

Lack of Interest

Some board members have absolutely no interest in raising money. One key element in changing this is to expand the types of fund development activities we ask board members to be involved with. This could include calling current donors to say thank you – or writing a personal note.

The moment for mission we talked about early is one way to overcome this challenge – especially when it shows a clear link between funds raised and the impact your programs have on people's lives. Engaging board members in the direct work of the organization is another way to connect people more closely with that positive impact.

An outside person coming in to speak brings a fresh voice to your board. They might say the exact thing you've been saying for years, but they listen because it's an outside 'expert.'

The best way, of course, is to ensure that the interest is there from the beginning. During the recruitment process, ask questions to make sure that your potential member is indeed passionate about your cause – and not just trying to fill out their resume.

Be patient with this process – especially if you are trying to transform the culture of a board that has been operating for a while with limited involvement in fundraising. It can take several years to recruit new people who are eager to be involved in raising and growing funds for your organization.

Lack of Knowledge

Lack of knowledge is one of the easier challenges to address. People are sometimes afraid of what they don't know about, so providing training can help increase comfort level.

Inviting members to share their success stories related to asking for gifts can be instrumental in teaching through example.

Partnering people who are newbies to asking for money with people more experienced can also help.

And, let people ease their way in to the process by becoming involved in stewardship of current donors. There's nothing like talking to a donor to (1) get re-inspired about the programs you offer and (2) realize that asking for money isn't about the money at all.

Fear

Perhaps the challenge is a general sense of fear of the unknown.

Again, try to ease people in – especially if they've been involved with the program for a while and have never been expected to ask. Thanking donors through phone calls and handwritten thank you notes is a great place to start.

Make sure that people know that asking for support is not about begging – it's inviting people to be part of a cause that they are already passionate about.

Providing a sample script can also take away some of that fear of the unknown. Having a list of 10 most frequently asked questions (along with answers to those questions) is another big help.

Again, partner newcomers to asking for gifts with someone more experienced, and provide training or coaching to help them get started.

Structural Barriers

In some cases, the structure of the board itself is not conducive to fundraising success. I'm sure you don't believe this, but there are some boards that have never been told that involvement in fundraising is part of the expectation for serving on the board. In that case, plan on making some changes to your job description and in the recruiting process.

I've run in to some cases where the board is appointed, rather than selected. There are two options for addressing that – one is to just go ahead and add a fundraising committee that is recruited – rather than appointed. The second option is to find one or two people on the board who are interested. Work with them to do everything you can to ensure that they are a success. Then ask them to share their experiences with the rest of the board. Enthusiasm is contagious. It might take several months, or even a couple of years, but one or two additional members will come around – then one or two more. Don't expect it to change overnight, but with consisted pressure over time, this can be turned around.

The third structural difficulty I've seen is that the Development Director or Chief Development Officer is not even invited to board meetings. As income is essential for programs to operate, adding fundraising to every meeting's agenda is also essential. The fundraising committee chair will most likely be presenting the information, but the development director also needs to be there as a resource. In addition, the Development Director will be building relationships with board members so that they are better able to engage them in the fundraising process.

Key Points

- Provide clear expectations up front.
- Provide resources to make the job of your fundraising team as easy as possible.
- Develop SMART goals together – that is: specific, measurable, attainable, realistic and timely.
- Provide regular reports so that everyone can see your progress.
- Provide feedback – and encouragement on an ongoing basis. Take some time to celebrate your small accomplishments to help keep momentum going.
- Lead by example – and support your leaders so that they in turn can lead by example.

15706243R00070

Made in the USA
Lexington, KY
12 June 2012